FARTING

RIPPER, TOOT, VAPOR, WIND, PASSING GAS...
A FART BY ANY OTHER NAME WOULD NOT SMELL AS SWEET!

By Barry Seltzer
and Erwin Seltzer

Prism Publishing Inc.

Also by Barry Seltzer
It Takes Two Judges To Try A Cow

Barry and Erwin Seltzer

To my trusted paralegal, Marilyn Dichter, without
whose continuous pushing and shoving, all the parts
of this book would still be floating in cyberspace.
...Barry

FIRST EDITION

Library of Congress Catalog Card Number 98-065706
Seltzer, Barry.
  Farting: Ripper, toot, vapor, wind, passing gas...a fart by any other
  name would not smell as sweet! / Barry Seltzer & Erwin Seltzer.

  ISBN 0-9664313-0-8
  Includes index
  1. Education.   2. Humor   I. Seltzer, Erwin   II. Title

1999

Heralded as "the King of the Airwaves" by the *Unfortunate* magazine, Barry Seltzer is the premier aromatherapy guru; his national mediocre-seller *It Takes Two Judges To Try a Cow* identified the judicial trends that defined the decade, from the courtroom to the phenomenon of flatulence. Nobody has been more accurate in demonstrating how to profit from these trends, and in *Farting*, Seltzer tells the readers how to apply the knowledge gained from understanding gas production to more recently identified trends that fit the lifestyles associated with well-being and natural living.

The man who went beyond the seriousness of the courtroom, who predicted the obsession with bodily functions, now shows readers how they can actively use their new understanding in their personal and business lives. From trying a cow to exploring the Ethernet to taking the aromatherapy approach, *Farting* guides the reader through the cultural millennium.

Seltzer and his co-author, Erwin Seltzer, sniff out the oldest and latest airy information, that Seltzer's company, Seltzer, Dichter & Seltzer, has identified through extensive surfing on the Internet. To illustrate the subject, Seltzer and Seltzer talk about people they've interviewed, read about and heard of and give examples of new styles and new techniques, as well as individuals who have successfully farted.

Farting is an invaluable road map that will teach readers how to be at ease with a taboo subject and enjoy the process. It is about changing winds, having a gas and coming up smelling of roses.

Barry Seltzer wishes to be retired from his real estate law practice, which services the Unfortunate 500, whose clients include Abe Laroux, Pepi Lepew. A nationally known speaker, radio and TV guest, he is co-author of *It Takes Two Judges To Try A Cow*. He lives close to the 49th parallel, somewhere between Ottawa and New York.

Erwin Seltzer wishes to be retired from his matrimonial law practice, which also serves the Unfortunate 500, whose clients certainly don't want to be named in this book.

CONTENTS

Flatulence in Literature

In the Media

The scientific poop on farting

Anecdotes of Flatulence

Flatulence and the Greenhouse Effect

Products

INTRODUCTION

I first became interested in the subject of farts, and farting, while researching my first book, *It Takes Two Judges to Try a Cow* - a compilation of bizarre legal cases. One day I read about a humorous incident involving flatulence that took place in a US courtroom. Intrigued, I began a more thorough inquiry of the subject.

I soon realized that flatulence makes its way into many areas including literature, history, medicine and the market place. I raided the few books other brave souls had written on the subject, the most genteel of which is a slim volume by Canadian writer Munroe Scott. I haunted the library and the Internet looking for additional material. During the course of a year I uncovered more information about the subject of farts and farting than I thought possible.

With the help of my brother Erwin, my colleague Marilyn Dichter and the folks at the Art Works, I have at long last been able to put these stories and anecdotes together.

Many people are uncomfortable with this topic. I believe it is likely the last taboo. Hopefully this collection will amuse, entertain, enlighten and inform the reader and deliver the subject matter into the realm of acceptability.

FARTING
AND THE LAW
(Habeas gaseous)

While members of the legal profession are often thought of as long winded stinkers, they are not generally associated with the actual biological function of farting. Nevertheless, my initial interest in the topic of this book took shape when I stumbled on several court cases in which farting played a prominent role. I would like to start this book where I began, with a collection of unusual tales dealing with farting and the law.

I object, Your Honor. I really object.

The very first story I collected concerned a lawyer named Clark Head, in Calaveras County, California, USA. Mr. Head accused his opponent, Tuolumne County district attorney Ned Lowenbach, of repeatedly passing gas during a four-week jury trial.

"It was disgusting" proclaimed defense attorney Head, who represented burglary suspect Gary Davenport. After Davenport's conviction, Head threatened an appeal based on Lowenbach's "misconduct."

Head, said the prosecutor, passed gas "about a hundred times. He even lifted his leg several times." Lowenbach apparently apologized once, claiming he farted accidentally, but he continued to have a series of similar accidents.

Head claimed this was a sign of disrespect for him, his case and his client. He said in fifty jury trials he had "never seen anything like this."

The defense counsel protested the tactic on the record after the DA broke wind several times during the defense's closing argument, causing the jury to break into guffaws.

The court overruled his objection.

✧✧✧

Please blow into this balloon, sir.

Once I decided to look for other incidents in which the act of farting intersected the law, I was amused to find that in Anchorage, Alaska, a member of the state assembly introduced a private member's bill to prohibit "flatulence, crepitation, gaseous emissions and miasmic effluence." Had it passed, it would have made farting in a public place a misdemeanor, punishable by a fine of one hundred dollars.

Fortunately, private members' bills seldom become law, but had this one made it into the books, it could have precipitated a windfall, so to speak, in revenues for the state government.

Of course, the state would have had to first deal with the problem of enforcement. Would local police have been asked to keep their noses to the...er...grindstone, to detect violators? Or would the state have modeled a special group after, say, the parking authority, to sniff out culprits and issue tickets?

Would members of the flatulence patrol have been equipped with special detectors, perhaps farto-meters? How would they tell who, in a public place, actually committed an offense? Would they have had to capture a sample of the offensive smell and then take sample farts from everyone in the immediate area to compare composition and toxicity in a special fartology laboratory?

"Just blow up this balloon, sir. No, from the other end, sir."

Would they have introduced a sliding scale for fines? You know, higher fines for really toxic and pungent farts? Would they have charged family, friends, neighbors, restaurants or anyone else who might have contributed to the perpetrator's crime by fueling him, or her, with beans, cabbage, sprouts?

Would repeat offenders have been charged under environmental laws? Would there have been jail terms? Would they have lost their freedom to choose what to eat?

"Oh, please, Your Honor, must I give up cabbage rolls too."

✧✧✧

Toll, please

While I was delving deeper into the subject of farting and the law, I came across this curious snippet from the French village of Montluc.

It seems that many years ago, village law compelled prostitutes entering the hamlet for the first time to pay a toll. They had a choice of currency — four denarius cash, or one fart.

I'm sure there must be more to this story than meets the eye, but I was unable to obtain any further information.

✧✧✧

Jury duty a gas

I've always thought that serving on a jury would be a bit of a noble yet inconvenient obligation, but as this transcript from an American court case illustrates, doing your civic duty can really stink.

The court: I have a communiqué from the jury.

Defense Counsel: Number four again?

The court: I heard this sort of rumble over there earlier this afternoon and the jurors sort of looked strange. Well, it seems for the last week-and-a-half he has been passing gas like mad in the jury box, and the jurors are rather upset about it.

Defense Counsel: I don't know if we need this on the record.

The court: This has been going on for a week and a half. A couple of them asked if their seats can be moved, but there are only so many seats in the box and he is right in the middle. I don't know whether we can seat him somewhere across the room or something.

Defense Counsel: Shall we go off the record?

The court: Counsel have agreed that we will resume for the next half an hour today, finish out the day, and at the end of the day the clerk will excuse Juror number four and tomorrow morning we will sit an alternate.

Some guys will do anything to get out of jury duty.

✧✧✧

Two more strange tales from the courts

In another incident from American law, an attorney had finished addressing the jury and returned to the counsel table when a sulfurous aroma invaded the courtroom.

"Dave!" his assistant whispered.

"Did you...?"

"I don't think so."

They glance at the judge, who shook his head and said, "Not me."

"Sorry" said the foreman of the jury.

Jurors and jury foremen are not the only parties afflicted.

In a second incident, Judge Joseph Addison remembers the time he asked a defendant how he pleaded to a criminal charge. The man replied with a loud fart.

Attorney, Tommy Horkins, to his feet and remarked:

"I'm sure I speak for all counsel present when I state that we hold a much higher opinion of your Honor than that expressed by the accused."

✧✧✧

I shall return.

And then there was the cheeky defendant who took preventative measures against a possible future infraction.

Prosecutor John S. Alexander tells the story of a farmer who was transporting produce to the town of Goderich, Ontario. En route, he found himself traveling the wrong way on a one-way street in heavy traffic — with no exit in sight. The problem was, he needed to pee. He finally leapt from his truck and urinated on the spot.

Unfortunately, a sharp-eyed policeman charged him with indecent exposure. The farmer was convicted, but the sympathetic judge went easy on him, levying a light fine of eighteen dollars, including court costs.

The defendant handed a twenty-dollar bill to the court clerk and headed for the door.

The judge reminded him that he had two dollars change coming.

"Keep the change, Your Honor," the farmer muttered. "Someday I may have to fart!"

✧✧✧

Trouble at the Fart Mart

Now to the USA, where Jeff and Marty were co-workers in a grocery store. All was not well in the relationship, however.

Jeff complained that Marty continually, intentionally and repeatedly passed gas in his (Jeff's) direction. Marty, Jeff said, would hone in on him from across the room, sidle up, take aim and let one go.

US courts have occasionally heard air-quality lawsuits, but this was different. Jeff, unable to find an attorney to take his case, decided to act on his own behalf. Word about the trial spread, and on the hearing date the courtroom was jammed to the rafters

Jeff failed to attend. The judge dismissed the case noting he probably would have done so anyway had the plaintiff attended. Marty's behavior may have been "juvenile and boorish" said the judge, but there did not appear to be a law on the books against it.

❖❖❖

Just re-enacting the crime, Yer Honor

The Eau Claire Leader-Telegram of December 3, 1994, reported that a jury in Ellsworth, Wisconsin, deliberated for three hours before ruling against Stewart Blair in his lawsuit against his friend Maurice Poulin for injuries suffered when Blair tripped over a snowplow blade. Blair said Poulin caused the fall when he startled Blair by accidentally passing gas in his face.

In a postscript to the trial, as the jurors ceremonially exited the courtroom, the foreman audibly farted as he walked by the judge.

❖❖❖

Calling Florence Fartingale

The following story does not concern a court of law, but rather a professional association disciplining one of its own. The story takes place in Ontario, Canada, where a nurse was found guilty of professional misconduct for deliberately breaking wind in the presence of a patient's wife.

The first incident could have been an accident, but then, the victim told the discipline committee, the rude nurse asked her if she "wanted more" before letting go again. The accused claimed she couldn't remember the incident. She did, however, agree that it is impolite to pass gas in front of others.

She was suspended for six months for "vulgar and offensive behavior."

A published summary of the nurse's case lists a series of "indiscretions" over a two-year period, including slapping a co-worker on the bum, threatening to put another in a casket, and making offensive remarks about another colleague's sex life. Apparently, her patients weren't treated any better.

✧✧✧

And finally ...

The most famous lawsuit, where a fart was the subject matter of the suit, blew up in France many years ago, when the "Moulin Rouge" launched an action against one of its most famous contract performers, a man named Joseph Pujol. I have left the details of this long-winded and complicated story for inclusion in the chapter entitled Anecdotes on Flatulence, "Le Petomane."

✧✧✧

ROOTS
(-a-ṭoot-toots)

As I began rummaging for references to this most arcane of subjects, I began to wonder why it was, in fact so arcane. There are lots of references to other body functions in almost every facet of human endeavor. But references to this one are rare, indeed.

I concluded that what it all boils down to is attitude. I decided to explore our modern attitudes toward the humble fart, and speculate on the reasons for them.

I can too!

Back in the 1970s, Texas Democrat, Lyndon Baines Johnson, the 36th President of the United States, confirmed what many of us already suspected about Gerald Ford, the bumbling Republican who served as Richard Nixon's Vice-President and eventually became President himself when Nixon resigned.

"So dumb he can't even walk down the street and chew gum at the same time," Johnson is said to have drawled.

But that's not exactly the phrase Johnson uttered. Some zealous guardian of good taste in either the White House, or the media, censored the President's real pronouncement, which was the shorter, if not sweeter: "So dumb he can't even fart and chew gum at the same time."

The lesson? Even in the decade after the "let-it-all-hang-out" Sixties, the American public wasn't deemed ready to hear that their president used the word fart. They were ready for news clips of the war in Viet Nam with supper every evening; they were even ready for that other f-word, which was cropping up more and more in the media, but they were not ready for the word *fart*. It is interesting to note that 30 years after President Johnson's censored comment, the American public has become extremely liberal and forgiving about the actions of their president.

✧✧✧

Who flatted?

If nothing else, the Johnson-Ford incident illustrates our baffling aversion to that innocent, 600-year-old, four-letter word *fart* and the entirely natural and healthy bodily function it represents. Almost no other word in the language is as ostracized or as lonely. Most dictionaries omit it. Those that don't, shun it as vulgar, without supplying a polite synonym. That's because they can't. There isn't one.

English comprises the largest vocabulary of any language ever spoken — more than a million words. It embodies thousands of synonyms. It houses dozens of words to replace the adjective *big,* for example, or the verb *to travel.* It even has two reasonably polite words for expelling gas through the mouth (*belch* or *burp*).

But this majestic language of ours contains only one puny, four-letter word — a vulgar one at that — to describe the expulsion of intestinal gas through the anus (verb), and to name the gas once it has been expelled (noun).

11

What about *flatulence,* or *flatulent* (Latin: flatulents — a blowing)? Sorry, these words describe the condition of having gas in the intestines. And there is no verb form. Ever hear anyone ask: "Who flatted?"

Of course, there are coy ways around the vulgar f-word. We pass gas. (Pass it to whom?) Or we *let one rip, break wind, cut the cheese, step on a duck* (quaaak), talk with the *wrong mouth, spark, toot* or *poot* (poot?) — depending on the local idiom. Nouns are scarcer, but the terms *raspberry, Sneaky Pete* and *cheek slapper* spring to mind.

What is amazing is that while that other disreputable f-word perches, ready to fly at a moment's notice on so many tongues, including politicians and the media, *fart* is still an illegitimate child, a mot terrible, a social outcast, an ill wind that blows no good.

While the Oxford English Dictionary snootily declares the word *fart* to be "not in decent use," it has not always been thus. I discovered that the word was perfectly respectable from the fourteenth century to the mid-eighteenth century. It was used, for example by the great English poet Geoffrey Chaucer in the Canterbury Tales, written in the late-1300s. Other poets and playwrights used it freely and legitimately through the ages.

For those of you who are interested in the evolution of language, the word can be traced to the Indo-European mother tongue of many ancient and modern Europeans. To oversimplify a complex process, the Indo-European word for fart was *perd*, which became *pedere* (to fart) and *peditium* (a fart) in Latin. Like many Latin words, the p became an *f* and *d* became *t* in the Germanic tongues, including English. Words, such as *pater* became *father*, and *duo* became *two*. After centuries of evolution, the Indo-European *perd* became *fert* in English, finally emerging as *fart*. At various times through the ages it has been spelled *fert, ferte, fartt* and *farte*.

Perhaps if the 'e' had remained at the end of the word, it would have appeared more genteel and thus remained in good taste.

✧✧✧

You baked what?

While we shun using the word *fart* to describe the particular bodily function it was meant to describe, we have no hesitation in appropriating it for other uses. For example:

"Stop farting about (wasting time)."
"Don't mind him, he's an old fart (a worthless person)."
"He doesn't give a fart for his family (cares nothing)."
"You have about as much chance as a fart in a wind storm (no chance at all)."
"He's the president's fart-catcher (errand boy or toady)."

Strangest of all? In the 1500s, a light pastry puff was called a fart. Next time your mother or wife bakes puff pastry, by all means, demonstrate the depth of your knowledge of the English language. Bite into the pastry, chew slowly, savor the flavor and then exclaim wisely: "Ummmm. Nice fart, my dear."

How this pastry came to be known by such an indelicate name is the subject of a legend. Hundreds of years ago, a young nun farted while cooking a meal at the Abbey of Marmounter in France. Some other nuns heard the fart and burst out laughing; and the young nun was so embarrassed that she dropped a ball of dough into a pot of boiling oil, where it immediately expanded into a fluffy golden nugget. Another nun fished it out and ate it, it tasted so good that the nuns prepared all of the dough that way. The little doughnuts - christened *pet de nonnes* or *nun's farts* became so popular that the Old English word *farte* became synonymous with balls of light pastry.

✧✧✧

13

Farting around the world

While the English language is relatively impoverished when it comes to words to describe the expulsion of intestinal gas, other languages are less stingy. Many have several words, depending on the type of fart being named, and both verb and noun forms. Here then, is a linguistic mini tour of farting around the world.

Afrikaans	(n) (v)	poep, maagwind, skeet, windlet
Albanian	(a)	mfryet (Same to you, fella.)
Algerian Darja	(n)	Hezga (a fart) Tecca (a fart) Hezzaag (someone who farts)
Arabic	(n)	eegayas (loud) eezarat (soft) eefessy (loud but odorless)
Austrian	(n) (v)	Schass (a fart) Koffer (a fart) anobstellen (to fart) koffern (to fart)
Azerbaijan	(n)	Osturag (a fart)
Bantu	(n)	lu-suzi
Belorussian	(v)	Bzdzec (to fart with smell) Piardzec (to fart)
Bobabgi	(n) (v)	mokinya ta monkinya

14

Breton	(n)	Bramm (a fart)
Catalan	(n)	Pet (a fart)
Cantonese	(n)	fong
	(v)	fong p'ayee
Cornish	(n)	bram (pl., bremmyn)
	(v)	Bramme, Vramme
Crow	(v)	piaky, pi, piahi
	(a)	nadmuty, nabubrely, nafoukany
Danish	(n)	fis, skid
	(v)	fise, sla en skid, slippe en vind
Dutch	(n)	scheet, wind
	(v)	een scheet, een wind laten
		brockkoesten
		reutelen
Esperanto	(n)	furzo
	(v)	furzi
Finnish	(n)	pieru, ilma, vatsassa
	(v)	pierra
French	(n)	pet (pronounced "pay"), vesse (silent but deadly), pet foireux (nervous and wet), pet de macon ("Mason's fart," i.e., leaves mortar), pet de nonne ("a nun's fart" = a pastry that hisses when it hits the grease), pet de negre (choco late pastry), prout (children's

		term, a "boo-boo"), petole (fart with a lump) peteur (male farter) peteur (feamale farter) petarade (series of animal farts)
	(v)	peter, lacher des vesses
Gaelic	(n)	braim, bram (often associated with raisins)
German	(n)	der Furz, der Pup
	(v)	furzen
Greek	(v)	perdomai
Guarani	(n)	Pyno (a fart, to fart) Tepyno (a fart)
Hawaiian	(v)	puhi'u (audibly) hio, puhihio, 'ohio (silently = revenge on the midwest?), pi (sputtcringly), 'enakoi (foully)
	(n)	pu'u puhi'u (urge to break wind) palale (sound of breaking wind)
	(a)	makani, palani
Hebrew	(n)	nuhfccchah
	(v)	hahfay-ach
Hungarian	(n)	koz, fing
	(v)	fingik, szellent, buzol
Indian (Hindi)	(n)	pud, vayu
Indian (Kannaras)	(n)	gali
	(v)	husu

Indian (Malayalam)	(n)	poochi
Indian (Tamil)	(v)	kasu
Indonesian	(n)	kentut, angin busuk
	(v)	berkentut
Italian	(n)	peto, scor (reggia)
	(v)	fare un peto, scor (reggiare),
	ruttare	
Japanese	(n)	he, hohi
	(v)	hohi suru
Kikuyu	(v)	thebea, thuria, eruka eruruka
	(compare with English	
		erucation, meaning "belch")
Korean	(n)	Pongu (a fart)
Lamba	(n)	uwususi
	(v)	uwususi
Latin	(n)	peditum
	(v)	pedere
Latvian	(n)	Pirdiens (a fart)
		Bezdals (a fart without sound)
		Bezdelis (someone who farts)
		Perdelis (someone who farts)
	(v)	Pirst (to fart)
Malay	(n)	kentut, angin, keleput (sound of breaking wind)
	(v)	ter kentut

Maori	(n)	Pihau (a fart)
Noewegian	(n)	fis, fjert
	(v)	fisc fjerte, slippe en fjert, slippe
el fis		
	(a)	ful av wind
Occitan	(n)	Pet (a fart)
		Vent (a fart)
		Vessinada (a fart)
		Lofa (a silent fart)
		Lofia (a silent fart)
		Vessina (a silent fart)
Persian	(n)	Gooz (a fart)

Philippines
  Tagalog, Cebuano,
  Samar-Leyte Bisayan: utot
  Bikol Pangasiun: atot
  Kapampangan, Ivatan: atut
  Ibanag: attut
  Ilkukano: uttot
  Magindaanaw: tut

Polish	(n)	pierdzenic, bzdziny, waitry (wind)
	(v)	perdziec, bzdziec (cf. Russ), Puszcac, waitry (release wind)
	(a)	wywolujacy
Portuguese	(n)	peido, gas intestinal
	(v)	expelir gases intestinais, peidar
Romanian	(n)	gaze, suflu
	(v)	sunflare
	(a)	a avea venturi

Russian	(n)	perdyozh (act of breaking wind) perdun (the outcome, also the perpetrator) perdil'nik (the place from whence it comes) Perun (the ancient god of wind) bzdun, bzdyukha (a silent fart, also a stupid jerk)
	(v)	perdet' (to do it with or without sound), bzdet' (to do it silently); the use of prefixes and suffixes is permitted: pereperdet' (to fart repeatedly, to refart), nabzdet'sya (to fart silently to complete satisfaction)
Saami	(n)	Buoska (a fart)
	(v)	Buoskut (to fart) Suooahit (to fart without sound) Busket (to fart once) Buskkas (farting) Buskolas (frequent farting)
Slovene	(n)	pezdec, ventrovi
	(v)	pezdeti, ventrovi imeti
Spanish	(n)	pedo, flato (Greek philosopher?)
	(v)	pedorrear, peer, ventosear, tirar un pedo (let one fly)
Swahili	(n)	Shuzi (a fart) Mashuzi (a fart) Shuta (a fart)
Swedish	(n)	fjart
	(v)	slappa sig

Swiss German	(n)	Fohn (a fart)
	(v)	Fohna (to fart)
Tarahumara	(n)	uii-re
	(v)	uii
Welsh	(n)	gwynt, yn y bol
	(a)	gwyntog, bolwyntog
Yiddish	(n)	nefikhe
Zulu	(v)	suz, shipha

THE ANCIENTS DID IT

(Farting around in the past)

As I began accumulating material for this book, I explored the past for references to the ignoble fart. Did the ancients acknowledge this lowly function? Did our more recent ancestors refer to it? Was their attitude toward it similar to ours? I turned first to the river valleys of the Tigris, Euphrates and Nile. It was a short visit. The cuneiform writings of the Assyrians, Babylonians and other ancient peoples of the area were apparently silent on the subject, as were the hieroglyphs of the Egyptians.

Was farting too unremarkable, or too crude, to make it into the official annals of the ancient Near East? Or, have modern archaeologists failed to report any references to such a lowly subject? How would one depict a fart hieroglyphically? The mind boggles.

Eat no beans

If the ancient Near Eastern civilizations failed to mention the fart in their writings, the ancient Greeks did not. Nothing was too insignificant or vulgar to escape their notice.. For example Pythagoras, the mathematician who proved that the square of the hypotenuse of a right-angle triangle is equal to the sum of the squares of the other two sides, advised his followers: "A fabis abstinetes," which means "Eat no beans."

✧✧✧

Hippocrates: Do it quietly

In about 400 B.C., Hippocrates, the father of modern medicine, turned his attention to the fart. The early Greek physician believed nothing happened without a natural cause and thus concluded that passing gas is necessary to well being.

Specifically, he wrote that farting is "a good thing if the gathering of wind moves down to the lower region... It is best to emit wind without a noise ... but it is better to emit it even with a noise than to repress or smother it."

Then he added a rather bizarre rider, saying that if a fart is emitted noisily, "it is a bad sign and indicates delirium," unless, of course, a person does it deliberately."

No wonder the subject has been much neglected by the medical profession over the past 2400 years.

✧✧✧

Et tu, Claudius

Now on to ancient Rome, where it is said that the emperor Claudius was the first to propose a law to deal with farting in public.

It would be easy to jump to the conclusion that such a law would be punitive, along the lines of, say, banishing any guilty party to live forever among the Germanic tribes.

Not so, according to Eric Rabkin and Eugene Silverman, who wrote *It's a gas: A study of Flatulence*. Apparently, the emperor, who is not usually remembered as a kindly man, proposed his law after hearing about a citizen so overcome by shame at having farted at a feast that he nearly choked to death. Not wanting anyone to risk death over such a trifle, Claudius was prepared to publish an edict permitting all people to fart at the table without suffering any penalty.

Claudius was either very tolerant or incredibly empathetic. In any case, according to one story, his wife fed him poison mushrooms before he could proclaim his law.

✧✧✧

St. Augustine invents another wind instrument

In an argument supporting free will, St. Augustine wrote in 411 A.D.:

"Certain human beings have natural endowments quite different than others and remarkable for their very rarity ... some people produce at will, without stench, such rhythmical sounds from their fundament (behind) that they appear to be making music even from that quarter." — City of God.

✧✧✧

Does she, or doesn't she?

In the less distant past, Marco Polo reported that when a woman was being considered as a potential wife for a Tartar Khan, she would first be sent to live with the wives of his underlords. If they found that she neither snored nor farted in her sleep, then she might make it to the Khan's bed. Who knew the Tartar Khans were so fussy?

✧✧✧

FLATULENCE IN LITERATURE

(Odes to odors)

Since the historical documentation on farting was thin, I turned next to literature. Were the great writers intimidated by this one, four-letter word? Not all of them, apparently.

Aristophanes: The farting clouds

The earliest Western humorist, whose complete works are preserved, is the Greek dramatist Aristophanes. In a play titled *The Clouds*, written about 423 B.C., he mocks poor old Socrates, who, as an atheist, had little time for the gods. The satire revolves around Socrates' school of philosophy. One fine day, Socrates and his students are discussing what might cause thunder and lightning. Not Zeus, Socrates insists, but the crepitations of the clouds.

In the following scene, the old skinflint Strepsiades, complains to Socrates about his foolish son, Phidippides, whose gambling debts are totally out of control. He wants his profligate offspring to learn law at Socrates' school, the Thoughtery.

Strepsiades meets Socrates, the head of the Thoughtery, for the first time and asks what causes rain, lightning and thunder.

Strepsiades: Oh! Earth! What august utterances! how sacred! how wondrous!

Socrates: That is because these are the only goddesses; all the rest are pure myth.

Strepsiades: But by the Earth! Is our father, Zeus, the Olympian, not a god?

Socrates: Zeus! what Zeus! Are you mad? There is no Zeus.

Strepsiades: What are you saying now? Who causes the rain to fall? Answer me that!

Socrates: Why, these, and I will prove it. Have you ever seen it raining without clouds? Let Zeus then cause rain with a clear sky and without their presence!

Strepsiades: By Apollo! that is powerfully argued! For my own part, I always thought it was Zeus pissing into a sieve. But tell me, who is it makes the thunder, which I so much dread?

Socrates: These, when they roll one over the other.

Strepsiades: But how can that be? You most daring among men!

Socrates: Being full of water, and forced to move along, they are of necessity precipitated in rain, being fully distended with moisture from the regions where they have been floating; hence they bump each other heavily and burst with great noise.

Strepsiades: But is it not Zeus who forces them to move?

Socrates: Not at all; it's the aerial Whirlwind.

Strepsiades: The Whirlwind! Ah! I did not know that. So Zeus, it seems, has no existence, and its the Whirlwind that reigns in his stead? But you have not yet told me what makes the roll of the thunder?

Socrates: Have you not understood me then? I tell you, that the Clouds, when full of rain, bump against one another, and that, being inordinately swollen out, they burst with a great noise.

Strepsiades: How can you make me credit that?

Socrates: Take yourself as an example. When you have heartily gorged on stew at the Panathenaea, you get throes of stomach-ache and then suddenly your belly resounds with prolonged rumbling.

Strepsiades: Yes, yes, by Apollo I suffer, I get colic, then the stew sets to rumbling like thunder and finally bursts forth with a terrific noise. At first, it's but a little gurgling pappax, pappax! Then it increases, papapappax! And when I take my crap, why, it's thunder indeed, papapappax! pappax!! papapappax!!! Just like the clouds.

Socrates: Well then, reflect what a noise is produced by your belly, which is but small. Shall not the air, which is boundless, produce these mighty claps of thunder?

Strepsiades: And this is why the names are so much alike: crap and clap. But tell me this. Whence comes the lightning, the dazzling flame, which at times consumes the man it strikes, at others hardly singes him. Is it not plain, that Zeus is hurling it at the perjurers?

Socrates: Out upon the fool! The driveller! He still savors of the golden age! If Zeus strikes at the perjurers, why has he not blasted Simon, Cleonymus and Theorus? Of a surety, greater perjurers cannot exist. No, he strikes his own temple, and Sunium, the promontory of Athens, and the towering oaks. Now, why should he do that? An oak is no perjurer.

Strepsiades: I cannot tell, but it seems to me well argued. What is the lightning then?

Socrates: When a dry wind ascends to the Clouds and gets shut into them, it blows them out like a bladder; finally, being too confined, it bursts them, escapes with fierce violence and a roar to flash into flame by reason of its own impetuosity.

Strepsiades: Ah, that's just what happened to me one day. It was at the feast of Zeus! I was cooking a sow's belly for my family and I had forgotten to slit it open. It swelled out and, suddenly bursting, discharged itself right into my eyes and burnt my face.

✧✧✧

Chaucer: The miller's tail...er...tale

The earliest mention of the fart I could find in English literature appeared in that old college favorite, the Miller's Tale, by Geoffrey Chaucer, who wrote it in the late 14th century as part of his Canterbury Tales.

Often omitted from expurgated editions of the classic collection, this bawdy story depicts jealousy and infidelity. The Miller's Tale is a truly funny, sort of a 14th century sitcom.

Here we have Old John, the jealous carpenter, who has married Alison, the prettiest 18-year-old in town. Living in John's household is the chore-boy, Robin, a maid named Jill and an Oxford student, who the Miller calls "handy Nicholas."

Nicholas has his eyes on Alison and is determined to get her alone. But the first trick is to get old John out of the way for the evening.

First, however, let's meet another character in the town named Absolon, the parish clerk, a musical randy dandy who has already seduced most of the women in the area and is determined that Alison will be his next conquest.

Here is how Chaucer describes the rakish cleric. [To sort out the Middle English of Chaucer, I turned to a translation of The Canterbury Tales by N. Coghill.]

"God bless my soul, he was a merry knave!
He knew how to let blood, cut hair and shave,
And draw up legal deeds; at other whiles
He used to dance in twenty different styles
(After the current school at Oxford though,
Casting his legs about him to and fro).
He played a two-stringed fiddle, did it proud,
And sang a high falsetto, rather loud;
And he was just as good on the guitar.
There was no public house in town, or bar,
He didn't visit with his merry face
If there were saucy barmaids round the place.
He was a little squeamish in the matter
Of farting, and satirical in chatter."

Despite his sophisticated caterwauling, Alison gave the determined cleric the cold shoulder, which made her even more desirable in his eyes.

Now, back to Nicholas and his truly bizarre master plan to get Alison alone for an evening.

First, he hangs out in his room for days, not making a sound. When Old John finally sends up to see if Nick is sick, the chore-boy finds the lodger sitting upright in bed, eyes and mouth open and apparently quite mad. Old John arrives to see for himself and Nicholas explains he has seen a vision of a second great flood.

Nicholas instructs the horrified landlord on what he must do to avoid catastrophe. First, he must not tell anyone about the premonition. Second, he must send the servants away. Third, Old John must secretly outfit each of three large kneading-troughs (one for himself, one for Alison, and one for Nicholas) with a day's supply of food. (The flood will come and go in 24 hours.) To maintain secrecy, the troughs should be hung up under the roof, accessible by ladder. Each should contain tools for cutting holes in the roof to escape when the water rises.

Old John bites like a trout and makes the preparations. Late Sunday, we find all three in their separate troughs praying silently to God to keep them safe. At least that's what Old John thinks.(Nicholas and Alison, of course, are spending the night in the bedroom.)

The plot thickens when Absolon shows up that very night outside Alison's window begging for a kiss.

Alison, perhaps egged on by Nicholas, lowers her bare bum into the darkness. While Absolon is no rocket scientist, he knows his cheeks, and the ones lowered for a kiss were not separated by a nose. Obviously irked, he rushes to a nearby smithy and quickly returns with a hot iron, calling artfully for another kiss.

In the meantime, Nicholas "has risen for a pisse," and plots to take Alison's little prank a step further. When Absolon calls for another kiss, Nicholas lowers his own behind over the window ledge. Tricking Absolon into kissing his rump would be a real corker all right.

Absolon, of course, can't see a thing in the darkness. He is fully expecting Alison to lower her bum again, but where is it? He calls for his love to speak so he can find his target. Nicholas responds in his own unique way. Let's return to N. Coghill's translation.

"Speak, pretty bird, I know not where thou art!"
This Nicholas at once let fly a fart
As loud as if it were a thunder-clap.
He was near blinded by the blast, poor chap,
But his hot iron was ready; with a thump
He smote him in the middle of the rump."

Poor Nicholas. All set for a harmless bit of humor, and winds up the victim of his own plot. The tale doesn't end here, but you can read it yourself to see how it all turns out.

29

Footnote: Chaucer's Canterbury Tales was one of many works that was banned for decades from the U.S. mails under the Comstock Law of 1873. Officially known as the Federal Anti-Obscenity Act, this law banned the mailing of "lewd," "indecent," "filthy," or "obscene" materials. Other items on the list included Aristophanes' Lysistrata, Boccaccio's Decameron, Defoe's Moll Flanders, and various editions of The Arabian Nights.

✧✧✧

François Beroalde de Verville:
A Frenchman in Rome

The works of François Beroalde de Verville (1558-1612) seem to have avoided the United States' Comstock Law. Beroalde is known best for his work, Moyens Parvenir (The Means to Success, 1610), a collection of off-color stories that has been suppressed for hundreds of years and never publicly printed in the United States.

Let's peek at one story from his famous collection, *A tale of Fair Imperia*. It tells what happened between the Sieur de Lierne, a gentleman of France, and a party girl in Rome just moments after they had risen from her bed.

She had put on a sort of pellicle, filled with sacs of nicely scented air. Equipped with these sweetly aromatic wind-bags, the fair Imperia listened to the gentleman's banter.

After a few moments, the lady reached down to one of the little bladders and made it explode. The gentleman heard the noise, and the red flag went up. Should he hold his nose?

'Tis not what you think," said she, "a man should know before he fears."

Suddenly, he smelled a pleasing odor: it was not what he feared. After several such incidents he asked where the sweet smells were coming from, since his experiences with French ladies had never been so pleasant.

She waxed eloquent on the wondrous aromatics of Italy, the lovely air and the like. Suddenly she let fly with another explosion -- this time of her own making. This time he should have held his nose. "Alas!" quoth he, "what is this?" "Tis a piece of courtesy," quoth she, "to put you in mind of your native land."

Jonathan Swift: The...ahem...Problem

Best known for his delightful satire, *Gulliver's Travels*, Jonathan Swift (1667 - 1745) also wrote the following poem, but it was not nearly so famous. Indeed, it was retrieved in the 20th century from manuscript.

The poem revolves around the question of who has been the lover of the Regent. His Lordship, it appears, emits gas as well as liquid at the most passionate moments. To get into his good graces, then, the ladies try to emulate the regal beagle.

The problem

Did ever Problem thus perplex,
Or more employ the Female Sex?
So sweet a Passion who cou'd think
Jove ever form'd to make a Stink?
The Ladys vow, and swear they'll try,
Whether it be a Truth or Lye.
Love's Fire, it seems, like inward Heat,

Works in my Lord by Stool and Sweat,
Which brings a Stink from ev'ry Pore,
And from behind and from before;
Yet, what is wonderful to tell it,
None but the Fav'rite Nymph can smell it.

But now to solve the Nat'ral Cause
By sober, Philosophick Laws,
Whether all Passions, when in Ferment,
Work out, as Anger does in Vermin?
So, when a Weasel you torment,
You find his Passion by his Scent.
We read of Kings, who in a Fright,
Tho' on a Throne, wou'd fall to white.
Beside all this, deep Scholars know,
That the main String of Cupid's Bow,
Once on a Time, was an Asses Gut,
Now to a nobler Officer put,
By Favour, or Desert preferr'd
From giving Passage to a Turd.
But still, tho's fixt among the Stars,
Does sympathize with Human Arse.
Thus when you feel an hard-bound Breech
Conclude Love's Bow-String at full Stretch,
Till the kind Looseness comes, and then
Conclude the Bow relax'd again.

And now the Ladys all are bent,
Ambitious of a Regent's Heart
Spread all their Charms to catch a Fart;
Watching the first unsav'ry Wind,
Some ply before, and some behind.
My Lord, on Fire amidst the Dames,
Farts like a Laurel in the Flames.
The Fair approach the speaking Part,
To try the Back-way to his Heart;
For, as when we a Gun discharge,
Altho' the Bore ne'er so large,

Before the Flame from Muzzle burst.
Just at the Breech it flashes first:
So from my Lord his Passion broke,
He farted first, and then he spoke.

The Ladys vanish, in the Smother,
To confer Notes with one another;
And now they all agree, to name
Whom each one thought the happy Dame:
Ouoth Neal, whate'er the rest may think,
I'm sure 'twas I that smelt the Stink,
You smell the Stink? by God you lye,
Quoth Ross, for, I'll be sworn, 'twas I.
Ladys, quoth Levens, pray forbear,
Let's not fall out; We all had Share.
And, by the most we can discover,
My Lord's an univeral Lover.

✧✧✧

Mark Twain: "I didn't write it!!!"

If you thought Swift was the only classic humorist to delve into the earthier side of the human condition, think again. *Tom Sawyer, Huckleberry Finn* and *A Connecticut Yankee in King Arthur's Court* may be better known than the piece that follows, but they were all written by the same irascible author, Samuel Clemens, aka, Mark Twain (1835-1910).

Written in 1876, between *Tom Sawyer* and *Huckleberry Finn, 1601* was part of a letter to Mark Twain's friend, the Reverend Joseph Twichell of Hartford, Connecticut. Twain prepared this sketch to "practice his archaics" after doing research for *The Prince and the Pauper.*
Twain denied authorship publicly at first, although he did admit that he wrote it in his later years.

1601

Despite its fine comedy, 1601 was suppressed for a quarter of a century after it was written because of its subject matter. When you read it, remember that both *and* and *an* sometimes mean *of* in Elizabethan English, and *ye* is a typesetter's abbreviation for *the,* and should be pronounced like the modern word *the.*

Conversation, as it was by the Social Fireside, in the Time of the Tudors.
[Date, 1601.]

[MEM.-The following is supposed to be an extract from the diary of the Pepys of that day, the same being Queen Elizabeth's cup-bearer. It is supposed that he is of ancient and noble lineage; that he despises these literary canaille; that his soul consumes with wrath to see the queen stooping to talk with such; and that the old man feels that his nobility is defiled by contact with Shakespeare, etc., and yet he has got to stay there till her Majesty chooses to dismiss him.]

Yesternight toke her maisty ye queene a fantasie such as she sometimes hath, and had to her closet certain that doe write playes, bokes, and such like, these being my lord Bacon, his worship Sir Walter Ralegh, Mr. Ben Jonson, and ye child Francis Beaumont, which being but sixteen, hath yet turned his hand to ye doing of ye Lattin masters into our English tong, with grete discretion and much applaus. Also came with these ye famous Shaxpur. A righte straunge mixing truly of mighty blode with mean, ye more in especial since ye queenes grace was present, as likewise these following, to wit: Ye Duchess of Bilgewater, twenty-two yeres of age; ye Countesse of Granby, twenty-six; her doter, ye Lady Helen, fifteen; as also these two maides of honor, to-wit, ye Lady Margery Boothy, sixty-five, and ye Lady Alice Dilberry, turned seventy, she being two yeres ye queenes graces elder.

34

I, being her maites cup-bearer, had no choice but to remaine and beholde rank forgot, and ye high holde converse why ye low as uppon equal termes, a grete scandal did ye world heare thereof.

In ye heat of ye talk it befel yt one did breake wind, yielding an exceding mightie and distresfull stink, whereat all did laugh full sore, and then-

Ye Queene.-Verily in mine eight and sixty years have I not heard the fellow to this fart. Meseemeth, by ye grete sound and clamour of it, it was male; yet ye belly it did lurk behinde shoulde now fall lean and flat against ye spine of him yt hath bene delivered of so stately and so vaste a bulk, where as ye guts of them yt doe quiff-splitters bear, stand comely still and rounde. Prithee let ye author confess ye off spring. Will my Lady Alice testify?

Lady Alice.-Good your grace, an' I had room for such a thundergust withinmine ancient bowels, 'tis not in reason I coulde discharge ye same and liveto thank God for yt He did choose handmaid so humble whereby to shew his power. Nay, 'tis not I yt have broughte forth this rich o'ermastering fog, this fragrant gloom, so pray you seeke ye further.

Ye Queene.-Mayhap ye Lady Margery hath done ye companie this favor?

Lady Margery.-So please you madam, my limbs are feeble wh ye weighte and drouth of five and sixty winters, and it behoveth yt I be tender unto them. In ye good providence of God, an' I had contained this wonder, forsoothe wolde I have gi'en ye whole evening of my sinking life to ye dribbling of it forth, with trembling and uneasy soul, not launched it sudden in its matchless might, taking mine own life with violence, rending my weak frame like rotten rags. It was not I, your maisty.

35

Ye Queene.-O' God's name, who hath favored us? Hath it come to pass yt a fart shall fart itself? Not such a one as this, I trow. Young Master Beaumont -but no; It would have wafted him to heaven like down of goose's boddy. 'Twas not ye little Lady Helen-nay, ne'er blush, my child; thoul't tickle thy tender maidenhedde with many a mousie-squeak before thou learnest to blow a harricane like this. Wasn't you, my learned and ingenious Jonson?

Jonson.-So fell a blast hath ne'er mine ears saluted, nor yet a stench so all-pervading and immortal.'Twas not a novice did it, good your maisty, but one of veteran experience -else hadde he failed of confidence. In sooth it was not I.

Ye Queene.-My lord Bacon?

Lord Bacon.-Not from my leane entrailes hath this prodigy burst forth, so please your grace. Naught doth so befit ye grete as grete performance; and haply shall ye finde yt 'tis not from mediocrity this miracle hath issued.

[Tho' ye subjoct be but a fart, yet will this tedious sink of learning pondrously phillosophize. Meantime did the foul and deadly stink pervade all places to that degree yt never smelt I ye like, yet dare I not to leave ye presence, albeit I was like to suffocate.]

Ye Queene.-What saith ye Master Shaxpur?

Shaxpur.-In the great hand of God I stand and so proclaim mine inocence. Though ye sinless hosts of heaven had foretold ye coming of this most desolating breath, proclaiming it a work of uninspired man, its quaking thunders, its firmament-clogging rottenness his own achievement in due course of nature, yet had not I believed it; but had said the pit itself hath furnished forth the stink, and heaven's artillery hath shook the globe in admiration of it.

36

[Then was there a silence, and each did turn him toward the worshipful Sr Walter Ralegh, that browned, embattled, bloody swashbuckler, who rising up did smile, and simpering say.]

Sr. W.-Most gracious maisty, 'twas I that did it, but indeed it was so poor and frail a note, compared with such as I am wont to furnish, yt in sooth was ashamed to call the weakling mine in so August a presence. It was nothing, less than nothing, madam- I did it but to clear my nether throat; but had I come prepared, then had I delivered something worthy. Bear with me, please your grace, till I can make amends.

[Then delivered he himself of such godless an rockshivering blast that all were fain to stop their ears, and following it did come so dense and foul a stink that which went before did seem a poor and trifling thing beside it. Then saith he, feigning that he blushed and was confused, I perceive that I am weak to-day and cannot justice do unto my powers; and sat him down as who should say, There, it is not much yet he that hath an arse to spare, let him fellow that, an' he think he can. By God, an' I were ye queene, I would e'en tip this swaggering braggart out o' the court, and let him air his grandeurs and break his intolerable wind before ye deaf and such as suffocation pleaseth.]

Then fell they to talk about ye manners and customs of many peoples...

Then conversed they of religion, and ye mightie work ye old dead Luther did doe by ye grace of God. Then next about poetry, and Master Shaxpur did rede a part of his "King Henry IV," ye which, it seemeth unto me, is not of ye value of an arsefull of ashes, yet they praised it bravely, one and all.

Ye same did rede a portion of his "Venus and Adonis," to their prodigious admiration, whereas I, being sleepy and fatigued withal, did deine it but paltry stuff, and was the more discomforted in that ye blody bucanier had got his wind again, and did turn his mind to farting with such villain zeal that presently I was like to choke once more. God damn this windy ruffian and all his breed. I wolde that hell mighte get him.

...

✧✧✧

Émile Zola: Peasant under glass

Émile Zola (1840-1902) wrote in the tradition called "naturalism," in which every little detail is recorded. Such writing often revealed the roots of social problems and sometimes brought them to the public's attention.

So, Zola's work was important as both an artistic and political accomplishment. In *La Terre* (The Earth), he focused on the peasantry and, true to form, he recorded every little detail. The following passage deals with a fellow named Jésus-Christ (no religious significance was intended), his father Old Fouran, his daughter La Trouille, and a bailiff named Vimeux.

Zola depicted these peasants as foul and boorish. Even worse, he joined in and treated it all as funny. Here is the beginning passage:

Jésus-Christ was a very windy fellow. Continual explosions blew through the house and livened things up. Damn it all, no one could ever be bored in that rascal's house, for he never let fly without blurting out some joke or other as well. He despised timid little squeaks, smothered between the cheeks, squirting out uneasily and ashamedly. He never emitted anything but frank detonation, substantial and ample as cannon shots. Whenever he raised his leg and settled himself with a comfortable and tactical motion, he called his daughter in tones of urgent command, and with a grave expression on his face:

"La Trouille, hurry, for God's sake!"

She rushed up and the blast went off point blank with such a vibrating energy that she gave a jump.

"Run after it. Get hold of it between your teeth and see if there's any knots in it!"

At other times, as soon as she reached him he would give her his hand. "Pull hard, draggle-tail! Make it go off with a bang!"

Then when the explosion occurred with the roar and splurge of a tightly-jammed charge, "Ah, that was a hard one, thanks all the same."

The piece goes on and on in the same vein.

✧✧✧

Sir John Suckling: Love's Offence

I remember as a young man, being told by someone much older, that the way to a woman's heart was through poetry. "Recite poetry to 'em and they'll be putty in your hands, " he said.

I have the feeling that the following poem, written by Sir John Suckling in the 17th century, was not what he had in mind, unless of course, you want to be dumped..

"Love is the fart
Of every heart:
It pains a man when 'tis kept close,
And others doth offend, when 'tis let loose."

Byron and Shelly: They both stink!

While one expects a certain amount of decorum from the truly great poets, alas, even they can be tempted, apparently, to pen verses more appropriate for the stall of a men's room. The following pair of two liners both entitled *Beans,* are attributed to Lord Byron and Percy Bryce Shelly respectively.

His Lordship's effort first:

"Beans they have the power to make one quite smelly
They make you smell worse than Percy Bryce Shelly."

Now Shelly's response:

"Beans, beans make your sphincter a siren
They make you smell almost as bad as Lord Byron."

Did the men who wrote Maid of Athens and Adonais really write these?

✧✧✧

Mozart's letters – in F# minor

Mozart was said to have written this letter to his cousin in 1777....

"...Oh, my arse is burning like fire! What on earth does it mean!--Perhaps some muck wants to come out? Oh yes, muck, I know, see smell you ...and...what is that? Is it possible...Ye gods! Can I believe those ears of mine? Yes indeed, it is so – what a long melancholy note!.... I stopped writing – I got up – went to the window...and...the sound ceased, I sat down again, started off again to write – but I had hardly written ten words when again I heard something. I got up again – As I did, I again heard a sound, this time quite faint – but I seemed to smell something slightly burnt – and wherever I went, it smelled. When I looked out of the window, the smell disappeared. When I looked back into the room, I again noticed it. In the end Mamma said to me :'I bet you have let off one.' 'I don't think so, Mamma,' I replied. 'Well, I am certain that you have,' she insisted. Well I thought 'Let's see', put my finger to my arse and then to my nose and – Ecce, provatum est. Mamma was right after all."

... and this to his mother in January 31, 1778.

"...Who carry their muck inside
And let it out, if they are able,
Both before and after table.
At night of farts there is no lack,
Which are let off, forsooth, with a powerful crack.
The king of farts came yesterday
Whose farts smelt sweeter than the may...."

I pass both along to you without comment.

✧✧✧

Arabian Nights: A thousand pardons, my love

Western writers were not alone in their making the fart a central fixture in the odd bit of writing. Oriental scribes were also willing. Consider, for example, a body of literature generally known as *The Thousand and One Arabian Nights*. An early French translation was first introduced to European readers in the first half of the 1700s, but it wasn't until about 1884 that a complete translation of all thousand and one tales had been translated from Arabic to English. And when all one thousand and one stories hit the press, it likely took a while before they discovered the stinker in the bunch.

Sinbad, Aladdin and Ali Baba became household names. Who can blame the readers of the day if they missed the tale

41

about Abu Hasan. As it happens, this is one of my favorite tales of the Arabian Nights.

Abu Hasan

It is related that in the town of Kaukaban, in Yemen, there was once a Bedouin of the Fadhli tribe called Abu Hasan, who, having given up the life of the desert and settled down as a townsman, became, after much diligence and enterprise, a merchant of considerable wealth.

His wife had died while they were both young, and his friends were always pressing him to marry again. Weary of the widower's life, he at length gave in to their persuasions and engaged the services of an experienced marriage-broker, who found him a bride as beautiful as the moon when it shines on the sea. He celebrated the wedding with a sumptuous feast, to which he invited his near and distant kinsfolk and friends and acquaintances from all over the countryside. His whole house was thrown open to the wedding guests. There was rice of every hue and flavor, sherbets, lambs stuffed with walnuts, almonds and pistachios, and a young camel roasted whole. Everyone ate, drank, and made merry; and the bride was displayed, according to custom, in seven different robes — and again in yet another robe as befitted such a grand occasion — to the great joy of the women, who marveled at her exceptional beauty.

At last came the moment when Abu Hasan was summoned to the bridal chamber. Slowly and solemnly he rose from this divan; but, horror of horrors, being bloated with meat and drink, he let go a long and resounding fart. The embarrassed guests, whose attentions had been fixed upon the bridegroom, turned to one another speaking with raised voices and pretending to have heard nothing at all. Abu Hasan was so mortified with shame that he wished the ground would open up and swallow him. He mumbled a feeble excuse, and, instead of going to the bridal chamber, went straight to the courtyard, saddled his horse, and rode off into the night, weeping bitterly.

After a long journey he reached Lahej, where he boarded a ship ready to sail for India, and in due course arrived in Calicut on the Malabar Coast. Here he met many Arabs, especially from Hadramaut, and was recommended by them to the King, who, though an unbeliever, took him into his service and in time promoted him to the captainship of his bodyguard.

He lived there in peace and contentment for ten years, and at the end of that time he was seized with a longing for his native land as strong as that of a lover pining for his loved one, so that he almost died of his self-imposed exile.

One day, unable to resist this yearning any longer, he absconded from the king's palace, boarded a ship, and eventually landed at Makalla in Hadramaut. Here he disguised himself in the rags of a dervish and, keeping his name and identity secret, traveled to Kaukaban on foot, enduring hunger, thirst and exhaustion, and braving a thousand dangers from lions, snakes, and ghouls. By and by he reached the hill which overlooked his native town. He gazed upon his old house with tears in his eyes, saying to himself: 'Pray God, no one will ever recognize me. I will first wander about the town and listen to the people's gossip. Allah grant that after all these years no one will remember what I did.'

He went round the outskirts of the town, and, as he sat down to rest at the door of a hut, he hears the voice of a young girl within, saying: 'Please mother, what day was I born on? One of my friends wants to tell my fortune.

'My daughter,' replied the woman solemnly, 'you were born on the very night of Abu Hasan's fart.'

When he heard these words, he got up and fled. 'Abu Hasan,' he said to himself, the day of your fart has become a date which will surely be remembered till the end of time."

He traveled on until he was back in India, where he remained in Exile until his death.

✧✧✧

The mist-descending flower-blossoming man

And just while we are in the Eastern world, let me assure you that Japanese writing is rife with tales of what Munroe Scott calls *The Vulgar Wind* in his book of the same name.

One such tale concerns a famous misemono performer, Kirifuri-hanasaki-Otoko, the "mist-descending flower-blossoming man." Misemono were variety shows that included all manner of strange and bizarre acts that flourished in Japan from about 1600 to 1870.

In an essay titled *Oh Farting*, published in 1777, Hiraga Gennai wrote:

"This prodigy of flatulence is unprecedented in the 2,436 years of this hoaryland of Japan...not only are these accomplishments unique in Japan, never has their like been heard from China, Korea, India, not even from the various states of Holland. What art! What farts!"

Kirifuri's act included something known as the farting scale, the Rosary Routine, the yoshiuara fanfare, the Kanoko curtain-raiser drum pattern, the No drum duet, an imitation of ballad styles, dogs barking, cocks crowing, and a simulated fireworks display.

Kirifuri performed in 1774 at the Ryogoku Bridge in Edo, the most well-known location for misemono events. He was described as a pale, plump, funny little man.

✧✧✧

IN THE MEDIA

As you might expect, the media is a wasteland when it comes to stories on gas passing, but occasionally an article or comment squeaks through, and the following is a compendium of selected items that have appeared in newspapers and on TV in the recent past.

Help! Lemme outa here!

Six Edmonton, Alberta, police cruisers chased and stopped a Loomis armored car in May after a report that it was weaving erratically on the road and that a guard appeared to be signaling by repeatedly swinging a door open. There was no holdup, according to police spokesman, Kelly Gordon; rather, one of the guards had passed gas, and the other guard was attempting to air out the cab.
– News of the Weird (September 27, 1996)

But Officer...

Kyle Krebs, a university freshman from Baylor University, was ticketed by campus police for passing gas. He received a citation for violating the campus ordinance against obnoxious odoros. Originally the remedial safeguard against smoke bombs and other noxious items. Mr. Krebs confirmed his flatulence was not directed at the campus police. With vehicular traffic in the area at the time he "never thought the decibel level would be so high" the officers would hear it. Mr. Krebs had the anti-odor ordinance ticket eventually dismissed.
– The Lawyers Weekly (July 24, 1992)

Between Bob and Bill

In response to a letter out of the CBS letter bag segment wherein a viewer asked David Letterman to advise him who to choose between Bob "pineapple" Dole and Bill Clinton, Letterman responded "I'm blank as a fart."
– The Tonight Show with David Letterman
(August 15, 1996)

Who knew?

"There's been a medical breakthrough. Flatulence can cure hiccups. Another example of the cure being worse than the disease."
– Jay Leno (July 10, 1996)

We are not amused

Richard Branson, founder of the Virgin music and airline empire, remembers that Diana, Princess of Wales, could grow pointedly funny about symbols of royalty. "She would often take the mickey out of Charles and the royal family," he recalls. "Once at a dinner party, a guest said to Diana, 'I know you don't like dogs.' 'Oh no,' said Diana. 'It's not dogs I don't like; it's corgis. They get the blame for all the farts.'" Corgis are the breed usually associated with Queen Elizabeth.
– Time (September 15, 1997)

Fifteen times a day?
A campaign by Netherlands Liver and Intestine Foundation to make breaking wind publicly acceptable. Fifteen times a day is about right, the group said.

Interstellar Gases

This exchange took place between Charles Duke and Jon Young during the Apollo 16 space mission in 1972. The astronauts did not realize that the media were listening.

Young: I got the farts again. I got em again Charlie. I don't know what gives them to me....I think it's the acid in the stomach, I really do.

Duke: It probably is.

✧✧✧

47

THE SCIENTIFIC POOP ON FARTING

(Natural gas)

We humans are not the only creatures who pass gas. Most of us know that dogs fart. Anyone who has spent an evening or two with old Bowser dozing in front of the fire, have had the Jeez-that-wasn't-one-of-mine experience while casting a baleful eye at man's best friend.

But, in fact, almost any animal with a digestive function also passes gas. Ants fart. So do termites, cats, and, of course, cows. All creatures great and small. Well, it's not altogether clear that ants and termites fart in the same sense we do. But they do expel methane gas as a by-product of their eating activities.

Although the act of passing gas is a common one, the medical and scientific communities haven't done much homework on the subject. They know little more than the bare mechanics. They don't understand much about why some people fart more than others, except that some foods make us more gaseous.

To prove my point, turn to the medical textbook Gastrointestinal Disease. In chapter 19, titled Intestinal Gas, in which authors Michael D. Levitt, M.D., and John H. Bond, M.D., state "...medical literature concerning bowel gas is relatively long on subjective impressions and short on scientific data."

✧✧✧

A passage from Merck

The Merck Manual is one of the driest medical dictionaries in the English language, but when it comes to farts, it slips into some (for it) thigh-slapping humor, consider the following passage:

"Flatus, which can cause great psychosocial distress, has been unofficially and humorously described according to its salient characteristics:

The 'slider' (crowded elevator type) which is released slowly and noiselessly with devastating effect.

The open sphincter or 'pooh' type which is said to be of higher temperature and more aromatic.

The staccato or drum-beat type, pleasantly passed in privacy."

✧✧✧

What is it, really?

Flatulence is the most common form of digestive disturbance. It is caused by swallowing too much air as may happen when talking too fast, eating or drinking too quickly, eating when anxious or upset or drinking carbonated sodas. The excess swallowed air passes into the stomach and gets trapped in the small intestine where, due to expansion, it stretches nerve endings causing that bloated uncomfortable feeling.

Another cause of flatulence is gas released when bacteria in the colon munch on the remains of undigested food. Over eating is a major cause of gas. When we over indulge in food we tax our digestive juices and enzymes. Without a sufficient amount of digestive secretions and enzymes in our stomachs, food can not be properly digested. Undigested food is a breeding ground for putrefaction which results in gas and bloating.

Diet plays a large role in gas production. Milk products contain a sugar called lactose which many people can not digest due to the absence of the digestive enzyme lactase. Beans are a common source of flatulence due to the presence of two sugars, raffinose and stachyose, which our digestive enzymes cannot break down.. Many high fiber foods such as cucumbers, apples, cabbage, and whole grains can be gaseous for some people. Some of the fiber remains undigested and then ferments in the large intestine. Fried foods and the concentrated sugars of dried fruit can also cause digestive disturbances.

✧✧✧

Relief

You can minimize gas by avoiding or reducing your intake of these gas producing foods: corn, potatoes, noodles, beans, peas, cabbage, asparagus, broccoli, brussel sprouts, dairy products, onions, artichokes, apples, pears, prunes, peaches foods containing the artificial sweetener Sorbitol, fried foods, pastries, rich sauces and gravies.

If you don't want to give up beans there are things you can do to make them somewhat "wind proof." Black-eyed peas, chick peas, and lima beans cause less gas than green beans, pinto beans and soy beans. Rinsing and soaking beans for atleast 4 hours before cooking in fresh water helps to remove some of their indigestible sugars that cause gas.

Slow down your talking, eating and drinking.

Sprinkle 3 to 10 drops of a product called 'Beano' on your beans. Beano contains the digestive enzyme we need in order to digest raffinose. Beano does not, however, reduce the gas found in milk or high fibre foods. Milk drinkers and dairy lovers can take lactaze pills just before they drink or eat to make dairy products digestible. They can also switch to lactase products such as Lactaid milk which contain the lactase enzyme. If that is

50

the culprit, you may have to try wheat free products available in health food stores.

Relief can also be found in supplemental form. Pantothentic acid and charcoal tablets are known to relieve intestinal gas.

Fermented foods such as yogurt and buttermilk aid in the digestion of high fiber and other food by promoting the growth of colon friendly bacteria.

Carminative herbs, such as fennel, ginger, garlic, anise, caraway, orange and lemon peel, stimulate the secretion of digestive juices thereby promoting digestion and decreasing fermentation.

✧✧✧

What's that smell then?

All of the five major gases in flatus are odorless. It's the trace amounts of ammonia, hydrogen sulfide, indole, skatole, volatile amines and short-chain fatty acids that create the smell.

Sulfur compounds (especially hydrogen sulfide, the rotten egg smell), produced by some foods, such as onions, leeks and garlic, are particularly noxious. When eaten with foods containing large amounts of indigestible carbohydrates, such as beans, yikes — instant room-clearing capability.

Ammonia is often a by-product of the digestion of the amino acids in meat, fish, and eggs, and from the digestion of glutamine in wheat. High-protein foods produce hydrogen sulfide and volatile amines.

51

Skatole is a special molecule whose name comes from the Greek word *skatos,* which means feces. And that's what it smells like. In fact, skatole is the particular molecule that gives feces its characteristic aroma. Indole, has a similar chemical structure and very nearly the same smell. It is generally produced with skatole when you eat foods containing tryptophan (an amino acid and one of the 21 building blocks of all the proteins in your body.) It occurs in almost all protein-rich foods such as eggs, fish and meat.

It is possible to reduce the smell of flatus somewhat by cutting down on high-protein foods and increasing the vegetable content of your diet. That is why the gas produced by vegetarians tends to smell less.

Remember, even if a fart smells bad, it doesn't mean you're sick, although it is true that in the Middle Ages, the scent of a fart was compared to the odor of the devil.

✧✧✧

Sound and fury

In addition to the odious assault to our olfactory sense, passing gas often produces a strange range of sounds, all of them embarrassing. Why are some farts louder than others?

The experts told me that the loudness of a fart is a function of the volume of gas expelled; the force used to expel it; and the presence of anatomical features, such as hemorrhoids, that could resonate. People with large hemorrhoids will likely fart more loudly than people with lax sphincters. Vegetarians, often fart quietly because the large, bulky stools they produce create looser sphincters. They will be detected socially only by the smell, whereas, carnivores may have less gas but, since they have tighter sphincters and may be more constipated, they will fart loudly.

All clear?

✧✧✧

How much is too much?

I expect most of us think we fart too much. That's because we seldom hear our friends and associates — or even strangers, for that matter — break wind. Therefore, we naturally assume that they seldom do it. Let's face it, we don't discuss things such as frequency or volume with other people.

The fact is, normal people, on a typical European or North American diet, produce between 200 and 2000 milliliters of gas per day, expelling it in an average of 14 to 21 small doses over each 24-hour period.

✧✧✧

What about the baby?

I understand that many mothers-to-be worry that the additional internal gas that often accompanies pregnancy will somehow affect the baby, perhaps causing the nipper to grow up with a phobia related to strong smells.

Doctors apparently agree that such fears are unfounded. The biggest risk associated with flatulence during pregnancy is mother's embarrassment. Doctors suggest that the condition can be minimized by eating smaller, more frequent meals, eating slowly, and avoiding gas-producing foods such as onions, beans, fried foods and members of the cabbage family.

✧✧✧

The bean factor

When a group of young men, in the service of science, feasted on a diet rich in pork and beans, farting increased from an average 15 milliliters to 176 milliliters per hour. Beans have a well-deserved reputation for increasing intestinal gas because they contain considerable amounts of those indigestible carbohydrates. Remember the rhyme from your childhood.

53

"Beans, beans, the musical fruit, the more you eat, the more you toot."

In World War II, it is said that Allied pilots were ordered to avoid eating beans because the reduced pressure at high altitudes caused their internal gas to expand, making them more fart prone. I presume the smell in the cockpit might have distracted them from their duties as soldiers.

✧✧✧

Another kind of fart-catcher

A British biologist who specializes in breeding peas and beans has invented a "flatometer" to measure flatulence. Dr. Colin Leakey (I'm not making this up) of Cambridge Peas and Beans Ltd. has devoted much of his career to finding what makes people pass wind.

The company is using his highly efficient chemical sniffing equipment (an improved version of a machine developed by NASA), to isolate elements that make people fart and then use the information to develop a windless bean.

Dr. Leakey has already produced one such non-flatulent bean, which he is testing on the French. But Leakey is now lamenting that he has been unable to get sufficient funding for his continuing studies on the causes of flatulence.

✧✧✧

Anatomical fart facts

It only takes 10 minutes for swallowed air to make it's way down to the large intestine, meaning that, as fart experts put it "Breakfast's food (and the gas it generates) gets there the same time as air from lunch."

54

Farts-to-be can sometimes actually be seen as dark cloudy areas on X-rays of the pelvis.

Morticians vigorously massage the corpse's lower abdomen to release any trapped, newly generated gas. In the past, neglect of this has resulted in the departed's farting during the open-casket viewing. (No mention is made of what happens to gas-filled corpses that are cremated.)

✧✧✧

Never in baseball

Apprentice baseball umpires are taught never to fart on the field, thereby losing the catchers' respect. (One would hope that apprentice catchers are taught the same thing.)

✧✧✧

Fish don't fart, why is this?

Fish do develop gas in the gut and this is expelled through the vent, much like that of most animals. The difference is in the packaging. Fish package their excreta into a thin gelatinous tube before disposal. This includes any gas that has formed or been carried through digestion. The net result is a faecal tube that either sinks or floats, but as many fish practice coprophagia, these tubes tend not to hang around for too long.

Most sharks rely on the high density lipid squalene to provide them with buoyancy, but the Sand Tiger shark, has mastered the technique of farting as an extra buoyancy device. The shark swims to the surface and gulps air, swallowing it into its stomach. It can then fart out the required amount of air to maintain its position at a certain depth.

✧✧✧

And astronauts?

Someone asked what happened when an astronaut farts in a space suit. According to the U.S. Airforce and Major Taylor - nothing. You don't smell it because the face cavity in the space suit helmet is overpressurized above that in the suit. All air flows from your face, into the suit and out through a release valve. However, anyone standing right next to you gets a pressurized blast of foul air.

✧✧✧

Curtail Fido's farting

If gas makes your pet a social outcast, it's time to seek a solution. Pets, like people, often have trouble digesting complex sugars in their food. Wheat, corn, oats and other grains are common offenders.

Because diet can create the problem, the solution may be as simple as switching pet foods. If this tactic doesn't work, or your finicky pet refuses to stop eating the offending food, consult a veterinarian. According to Calvin Clements of Palmyra, Pennsylvania, "Your pet may have more than a minor annoyance. Gas can also be a symptom of a serious colon disease."

Even if the diagnosis reveals that your pet simply has a gassy system, your veterinarian may be able to suggest a different diet or other remedies. For example, drops of a product called Curtail work by breaking down gas-producing substances when sprinkled on Fido's food.

✧✧✧

Rocking the pain away

Now this is a real home remedy. Research suggests the rocking chair may lessen the gas pain that usually occurs in moms who've undergone caesarean sections.

Researchers studied the effects of rocking along with modified diet medications and suppositories on 290 women who had just given birth by C-Section. Women who rocked 15 to 20 minutes at a time for a total of 60 or more minutes a day had fewer problems with intestinal gas than those who didn't. Rocking mothers also got up and around.

ANNECDOTES OF FLATULENCE

(Weird tales you don't want to relate to the kids)

Historians, journalists or other keepers of the public record have failed to take notice of the fart. Those stories and anecdotes that have been set down tend to be so unusual that they could not be ignored. Here is a collection of such stories.

Le Petomane

Joseph Pujol was born in Marseilles on June 1, 1857. While swimming as a lad, a rush of cold water entered his bowels through his anus. Alarmed, he consulted a doctor, who suggested he keep out of the water.

At age thirteen, Pujol was apprenticed to a baker, eventually setting up his own shop. In 1883 he married Elizabeth Henriette Oliver and subsequently fathered ten children.

While serving in the army sometime later, he remembered his childhood incident and discovered he could control the intake and release of water in his body by contracting his abdominal muscles. Later, using a basin, he practiced and mastered his water trick in private.

Once he mastered water, he tried air, discovering that, with practice, he could regulate sound. And there was no odor.

Returning home, he took up his old job as a baker for several years, but began moonlighting as a singer, trombone player and comic in music halls. Eventually, he incorporated his fart routine into his act. It was an almost immediate hit.

Yvette Guilbert, a popular chanteuse of the day, remembers the first meeting between Pujol and Monsieur Zidler, who booked acts for the Moulin Rouge. Zidler listened as the tall, sad-faced man explained that he was a 'phenomenon' and would soon be the talk of Paris.

"And what is your gift?" Zidler asked.

"Well, you see, Sir," his visitor explained in all seriousness, "I have a breathing arsehole..."

"Oh! Yes?" said Zidler.

"You see, sir, my anus is so elastic I can open and shut it at will."

"So?"

"So I can absorb any quantity of liquid I may be given."

When the basin was brought, Guilbert recalled, Pujol took off his trousers, to reveal a hole in his underwear at the necessary spot. Then, sitting on the basin, which was filled to the rim, he emptied and refilled it in no time.

"Ah, that's not all, sir... once I've been cleaned out in this way... I can expel an almost infinite quantity of odorless gas."

Zidler interrupted, "Let's keep it simple facts. You're telling me you can fart."

"Yes, ... but the unique thing about my act is the range of sound I can produce."

"You mean you sing through your rear?"

"Well... yes."

After Pujol demonstrated his tenor, baritone, bass light voice, vocaliser and one called the mother-in-law, Zidler hired him.

Audiences at the Moulin Rouge laughed and shrieked in hysteria as Le Petomane farted around on stage. As a finale, he invited everyone to join him in a group effort that brought down the house, at least figuratively.

By 1892, he was beginning his act with a spoken introduction, explaining his unique talent, and then moving on to imitations of occupational farts - a bricklayer, a nun and so on. Then there were the impressions, such as two meters of ripping cloth, the boom of a cannon shot and thunder. He later added barnyard mimicry.

He also left the stage for a moment and returned with a meter of rubber tubing sticking out of his rear. He placed a cigarette in the end and smoked it. Eventually he replaced the cigarette with a flute on which he played *Au Clair de la Lune*.

Finally, after removing the flute, he blew out the gas-fired stage lights, or a candle positioned a foot away.

People laughed and screamed hysterically. Women in corsets had to be taken away by nurses stationed in the hall. Pujol was a Paris sensation, pulling in more at the box office than leading artists. Sarah Bernhardt received eight thousand francs per engagement, while Pujol took home twenty thousand in an afternoon.

On the other hand, Pujol's contract with the Moulin Rouge imposed long working hours and restricted his performances outside the hall. Management wanted to maintain his exclusivity although he was allowed to travel abroad occasionally.

Regardless of his fame and fortune, he was a kindly man who loved his family and remembered his friends. His thoughtfulness led to what is likely the largest legal action ever based on a fart.

On one of his days off, Pujol dropped by an old friend's gingerbread stand at a local market. To help boost sales at the flagging business, Pujol performed a few simple acts to attract customers. Eventually, word of the impromptu performance traveled back to the management of the Moulin Rouge, fined him 3,000 francs for violating his contract. The Moulin Rouge launched a lawsuit when Pujol refused to pay.

While the Moulin Rouge won the suit, Pujol gained the freedom to set up his own traveling theater. Still, bitter about having to pay a fine for farting for a friend, he sought revenge.

✧✧✧

In the meantime...

...the Moulin Rouge, concerned about losing business to Pujol's theater, hired Angele Thiebeau, a female fartomaniac. When Pujol found out she was using a bellows to make the sounds, he sued her and the Moulin Rouge for fraudulent imitation.

That inspired a reviewer for the paper *L'art Lyrique et la Music Hall*, to report that Thiebeau's act was a cheap trick, devoid of skill, or any of Pujol's charm. Angele Thiebeau and the Moulin Rouge immediately launched a suit against the paper for defamation of character. Thiebeau said the paper had damaged her reputation and her ability to earn a living. Her only sin, she proclaimed, had been to use a contrivance in her act. Her lawyer alleged "the majority of physical feats produced in public places owe their effectiveness not only to skill but also apparatus and to tricks designed for illusion."

The Moulin Rouge and Thiebeau lost the suit against the paper. Pujol, satisfied with the disgrace of his old employer and the fraudulent imitator it had hired to replace him, withdrew his own suit against the pair despite the likelihood of its success.

61

World War I ended his long career. Depressed by injuries suffered by his sons, he never again performed publicly and returned to running a bakery and biscuit factory. He died in 1945 at age 88.

✧✧✧

A femme fartomaniac

While the trickster Thiebeau was an obvious fraud, one female fartomaniac may have been the real thing. La Mere Alexandre, who dressed like Pujol and toured the French countryside, imitated farts of the mason, the nun, the notary and the bombardment of Port Arthur.

She claimed her act was done without tricks or odors and was in good taste, even for women and children. Glib and confident, she charged no entrance fee for her shows, asking the members of the audiences to pay when leaving if they were happy with her performance.

✧✧✧

Ah...that crazy Japanese TV

For a modern day equivalent of Pujol, we must turn to Japanese TV in the early 1980s, more than 300 years after the amazing Kirifuri.

An unnamed performer appeared on the Two P.M. Show to produce a "tuneful, incredible repertoire" of crepitating sounds, according to a reporter for the Mainichi News.

The Asahi Daily News reported that the man claimed he could break wind 3,800 times in succession. To test him, the host of the show had him strip to his underwear and lay on the studio floor. A microphone was strategically placed to record the onslaught of sounds.

Later, the performer accompanied the studio orchestra on a song and for an encore, he attached a blowgun to his behind and short darts into a nearby target.

American reporters and writers were apparently indignant at the act. One suggested Japan, and not the United States may occupy the number one spot in TV vulgarity. Another wrote that laxative and feminine hygiene commercials, and shows such as The Dating Game and The Gong Show took a back seat to items on television in Japan.

Ahhh. There's that old American squeamishness again. Remember the re-write of Johnson's take on Gerry Ford?

✧✧✧

The royal fart (No, not Charles.)

Perhaps the most famous fart story in British culture involves not a performer, but royalty. It seems that Edward de Vere, Earl of Oxford, was to be presented to Her Majesty Queen Elizabeth the First, Queen of England and Ireland in the 1500s.

Upon introduction to good Queen Bess, de Vere dropped to one knee in supplication. His intestinal gases broke loose with a deafening report akin to the firing of a gun. Yes, he had farted in the presence of the Queen. Humiliated, he imposed upon himself a seven-year exile. (This is reminiscent of Abu Hasan in The Thousand and One Arabian Nights.)

When he returned to society, he was once again called on to meet the sovereign. When the Queen greeted him amiably and graciously, he figured that all had been forgotten. He was wrong.

The Queen whispered loudly: "My Lord, I had forgot the fart."

✧✧✧

Tinker, tailor, shoeshine boy

Then there is the story of the European tailor who farted loudly every time he bent over to measure the inseam of a client, startling both himself and his customer.

He harbored an overly developed cleanliness complex. He took offense in having to touch his customer's sullied shoes.

His uncontrollable farting was an unconscious, but aggressive, reaction to a situation he found detestable.

The prescribed treatment? He was to employ the services of a full-time shoeshine man who cleaned the shopper's shoes before each fitting. The "hire a shoeshine boy and call me in the morning" effected an immediate cure to the tailors aggressive farting.

◇ ◇ ◇

Roman noses

Martin Luther, the German cleric who fought with the Vatican, and ultimately started the Protestant movement, accused the Roman Catholic Church of spying on him so intently that "when I fart in Germany, they smell it in Rome."

✧✧✧

Ben Franklin's little joke

Benjamin Franklin (1706-1790) needs little introduction. He was, among other things, a printer, publisher, postmaster, inventor, writer and often a pain in the butt to his many detractors, which perhaps was why they were detractors.

The following letter was written by Franklin as a satire. To appreciate it's true bite, remember that the great man was a vegetarian. Aptly enough, Franklin directed the letter to the Royal Academy of Brussels — apt because the subject of the spoof often arises after the consumption of Brussels sprouts.

To the Royal Academy of Brussels

Gentlemen:

I have perused your late mathematical prize question, proposed in lieu of one in natural philosophy for the ensuing year... I conclude therefore that you have given this question instead of a philosophical, or, as the learned express it, a physical one, because you could not at the time think of a physical one that promised greater utility... Permit me then humbly to propose one of that sort for your consideration, and through you, if you approve it, for the serious inquiry of learned physicians, chemists, etc., of this enlightened age.

It is universally well known that, in digesting our common food, there is created or produced in the bowels of human creatures a great quantity of wind.

That the permitting this air to escape and mix with the atmosphere is usually offensive to the company, from the fetid smell that accompanies it.

That all well-bred people, therefore, to avoid giving such offense, forcibly restrain the efforts of nature to discharge that wind.

That so retained contrary to nature it not only gives frequently great present pain, but occasions future diseases such as habitual cholics, ruptures, tympanies, etc., often destructive of the constitution and sometimes of life itself.

Were it not for the odiously offensive smell accompanying such escapes, polite people would probably be under no more restraint in discharging such wind in company than they are in spitting or in blowing their noses.

My prize question therefore should be: To discover some drug, wholesome and not disagreeable, to be mixed with our common food, or sauces, that shall render the natural discharges of wind from our bodies not only inoffensive, but agreeable as perfumes.

That this is not a chimerical project and altogether impossible, may appear from these considerations. That we already have some knowledge of means capable of varying that smell. He that dines on stale flesh, especially with much attention of onions, shall be able to afford a stink that no company can tolerate; while he that has lived for some time on vegetables only, shall have that breath so pure as to be insensible to the most delicate noses; and if he can manage so as to avoid the report, he may anywhere give vent to his griefs, unnoticed. But as there are many of whome an entire vegetable diet would be inconvenient, and as a little quicklime of fetid air arising from the vast mass of putrid matter contained in such places, and render it rather pleasing to the smell, who knows but that a little powder of lime (or some other thing equivalent, taken in our food, or perhaps a glass of limewater drunk at dinner, may have the same effect on the air produced in and issuing from our bowels? This is worth the experiment. Certain it is also that we have the power of changing by slight means the smell of another discharge, that of our water. A few stems of asparagus eaten shall give our urine a disagreeable odor; and a pill of turpentine no bigger than a pea shall bestow on it the pleasing smell of violet. And why should it be thought more impossible in nature to find a means of making perfrum of our wind than of our water?

✧✧✧

Another reason not to smoke on an airplane

Passengers and crew on a South African Airways flight faced a different problem a few years back. The airliner, which was on its way to South Africa, was forced to turn back and make an emergency landing in Britain when its fire alarms started screaming.

Oh, there was no fire. It was all that heat and methane from the 72 farting pigs in the cargo compartment that triggered the alarms. Good thing no one lit up.

✧✧✧

"I was just looking for a quiet place to....errr...

A report that appeared in the New York Daily News November 1, 1994, told of a man, described as a career criminal being apprehended in the middle of a burglary at an upscale Fire Island, N.Y., home. The residents had gotten up to check out some strange noises but found no one. Near a closet door, however, they heard someone farting and discovered Richard Magpiong, 56, hiding in the closet. They held him until police arrived.

✧✧✧

Ta-dah --
Gustav Andre Stool, the famous farting ventriloquist

He was a famous nightclub entertainer of the late 1940's. During the late 1940's and early 50's he amazed audiences around the country with his ability to "throw" a fart across a stage and into the audience. By the middle 50's his act ran out of...ummm...steam. No longer in demand, he withdrew into seclusion.

67

Surfacing in the late Sixties, full of bitterness, he secretly toured the country embarrassing dignitaries and show business types by throwing his farts at inopportune times. His final "performance" came at the second inauguration of Richard Nixon. Standing in the audience, some 100 feet from the stand, Stool threw his fart right at Nixon right in the middle of the swearing in. At that moment the Chief Justice turned to a colleague and was heard to whisper, "An ominous air hovers over this administration."

✧✧✧

DANGER -- Natural Gas

Farting is generally not dangerous, however, I did discover some isolated incidents where injury and even death did occur.

One overweight man was killed by his fart. He was sleeping and farting in an unventilated room. The methane cloud that hung over his bed eventually killed him.

In another incident, a 13-year-old boy attempting to light a fart set his pants on fire.

Finally, during an intestinal operation, a spark from the operating instruments ignited the hydrogen in the man's stomach causing an explosion, he made a full recovery.

✧✧✧

Jack Dover's Quest of Inquiry -- Say again?

In a 1604 pamphlet called "Jack Dover's Quest of Inquiry", there is a section about a court jester named "The Fool Cornwalle." The section is as follows: I was told of a humorous knight dwelling in the same country, Corwalle, who upon a time, having gathered together in one open marketplace a great assemblie of knights, squires, gentlemen, and yeomen."

"While they stood expecting to hear some discourse or speech to proceed from him, he, in a foolish manner (not without laughter), began to use a thousand jesters, turning his eyes this way and then that way, seeming always as though presently he would have begun to speake, and at last, fetching a deep sigh, with a grunt like a hog, he let a beastly loud fart, and thold them that the occasion of this calling them together was to no other end but that so noble a fart might be honored with so noble company as there was."

✧✧✧

The Constipated Elephant

In Paderborn, Germany, overzealous zoo keeper Friedrich Riesfeldt, concerned about a constipated elephant named Stefan, gave the animal 22 doses of a laxative, more than a bushel of berries, figs and prunes and an olive oil enema before the plugged up pachyderm finally let fly and suffocated the zoo keeper under 200 pounds of poop.

Investigators say that while ill-fated Friedrich was attempting to give the ailing elephant the enema, the relieved beast unloaded on him like a dump truck full of mud. "The sheer force of the elephant's unexpected defecation knocked Mr. Riesfeldt to the ground, where he struck his head on a rock and lay unconscious as the elephant continued to evacuate on top of him", said flabbergasted Paderborn police detective Erik Dern. "With no one out there to help him, he lay under all that dung for at least an hour before a watchman came along." Unfortunately, help was too late and Friedrich suffocated. Detective Dern remarked," I had never really thought about it before, but obviously giving an enema to an elephant can be a very dangerous activity and not something that should be attempted alone."

✧✧✧

Surprise!!!!!!

Here's a story that could have happened – but then again it could also be an urban myth.

There once lived a man who had a passion for baked beans. He loved them, he adored them, he yearned for them. But they caused him a great deal of embarrassment. The reaction of his body was swift and terrible to behold. One day he met a girl and fell in love. When it became apparent that they would marry, he realised she might be embarrassed and humiliated by his addiction to baked beans. He decided to make the supreme sacrifice and give up his beloved baked beans. A short time later they were married.

Some months later, on his way home from work, his car broke down. He was not too far from home so he decided to leave the car and walk the rest of the way. He passed a small roadside cafe and decided to call his wife and tell her that he would be late for supper. As he entered the cafe, the smell of baked beans overwhelmed him. He still had several miles to go, and decided that he could walk off any after-effects before reaching home. Before he knew it, he had eaten three large plates of baked beans. As he got closer to home, the frequency and forcefulness diminished greatly, and he felt reasonably safe.

Just as he reached home, however, he felt a great rumbling inside and was seized with a terrible urgency. As he waited just outside his front door to release one last effort, his wife threw open the door. She excitedly exclaimed. "Darling, I have made the most wonderful surprise dinner for you." She blindfolded him and led him to his chair at the head of the table. Just as she was ready to remove the blindfold, the phone rang. She made him promise not to peek until she returned and went to answer the phone.

When she had gone, he seized the opportunity, shifted his weight to one leg and loudly broke wind. It was not only loud, but as ripe as a rotten egg. He had a hard time breathing, so he took his napkin and began to fan the air about him. He just started feeling better when he felt another urge. He again raised one leg and let her rip. It sounded like a tuba and smelled so bad that he started gagging. He fanned until his arms ached. Things had just about returned to normal when he felt another powerful urge. He shifted in his weight to the other leg and let go. This was a prize winner. The windows rattled, the dishes on the table shook and a minute later the flowers on the table were dead.

While keeping one ear on the conversation in the hallway he continued like this for the next 15 or 20 minutes, fanning away each time with his napkin. When the sounds of farewells indicated the end of the telephone conversation, he neatly laid his napkin in his lap and folded his hands on top of it. Smiling contentedly, he was the picture of innocence when his wife returned to the room. Apologising for taking so long, she asked if he had peeked. After assuring her he had not, she removed the blindfold, revealing the dinner guests seated around the table for his surprise birthday party.

FLATULENCE
AND THE GREENHOUSE EFFECT
(Not in my greenhouse, you don't)

When I first began to collect my little stories of farts and farting for my own amusement, I never really considered the serious side of the subject. It was only as I began to explore more deeply that I realized that there is a serious side. That men and women with scientific training have spent a good deal of their professional careers studying the consequences of human and animal releases of methane to our environment – their contribution to the greenhouse effect.

While carbon dioxide is one of the most abundant greenhouse gases in the atmosphere, methane and chlorofluorocarbons (CFC'S) actually have a much greater ability to trap heat. And where does methane come from besides decaying vegetation? It's produced in our bodies and expelled along with other gases in farts. And not just human farts either. Cows, pigs, termites — pretty much any animal with a digestive system — produce methane.

Indeed, some scientists say that developing nations — especially those dependent on livestock — contribute as much to the greenhouse effect as do wealthy industrialized nations. Among the top five contributors to global warming are Brazil, China and India, all relatively undeveloped.

✧✧✧

Holy cow!

The average adult cow apparently belts out about 162 litters of methane daily. That means the world's total cow population produces 120 billion litres of the greenhouse gas each and every day — enough to double atmospheric methane in the next century.

✧✧✧

More bull from the politicians

Despite the threat from farting cattle, U.S. News & World Report of November 5, 1990, failed to see the danger.

"We all like to take a poke at our politicians and the strange bills and laws that are passed but none is stranger than when United States lawmakers in their haste to get out of Washington, D.C. after one of their most embarrassing political seasons tucked into a bill a law to spend nineteen million dollars to study the methane emissions from the farting of cows and other barnyard animals. Isn't politics a gas!"

✧✧✧

If it smells bad, tax it

Every year, Australia's 24 million cattle and 150 million sheep put more than two million tons of methane into the atmosphere. That helps make Australia one of the world's five highest per-capita producers of greenhouse gases.

The Australian government has proposed taxing animal flatulence (yes, a tax on farting) as part of a proposal to cut greenhouse gas emissions by 20% by 2005.

73

That has prompted the animal health division of the Commonwealth Scientific and Industrial Research Organization (CSIRO) to develop a non-toxic compound, an antimethanogen, that suppresses methane production in cattle. Trials also got underway to see if the compound will work on sheep.

If the compound doesn't work, its back to the fart tax, presumably.

✧✧✧

Flatasaurus Rex, or Puff, the Magic Dragon?

Speaking of global warming, a recent annual meeting of the Geological Society of America discussed scientific findings that dinosaurs may have farted themselves into extinction. How so? The methane gas they emitted, may have helped warm prehistoric Earth's climate.

Now that's an extinction theory most of us haven't heard before.

Simon Brassell, a geochemist at Indiana University said "gas from dinosaurs included methane that may have been a minor contributor to global warming 75 to 80 million years ago". Eric Barron of Penn State University questioned the findings and commented "I wonder whether or not there were enough dinosaurs to make that substantial a contribution to atmospheric chemistry."

On the other hand, dinosaurs were so big, perhaps not many were needed to blow away the species.

✧✧✧

Got the munchies

Britain's Natural Environmental Research Council has estimated that farting termites are responsible for as much as a fifth of the world's methane gas. The council estimates that termites produce about 88 million tons of methane a year as they dine on trees and finished wood products, such as houses. "It's a lot of methane," said a spokesperson, "but there are a lot of termites."

This revelation about termites conjures up all sorts of bizarre mental images. Termites sprinkling Beano on logs before chowing down; termites standing around in a group with that "It wasn't me!" look on their little insect faces; teenage termites, with tiny Bics at the ready, eyeing one of their companions expectantly.

✧✧✧

Lots of Limericks
(There once was an urchin named Bart...)

Farting, like other basic biological functions, has long been the subject of tasteless limericks, jokes, and songs. While I don't pretend to possess a complete compendium of such items, my research did uncover a rather large sampling of limericks, and, a somewhat smaller number of other "humorous" bric-a-brac. Here then is a sampling of limericks, many of which have been around for a century or more.

The feminine mystique...

Most women do not find the passing of gas humorous, or even mildly amusing, and they don't understand why many men do. Indeed, many women react indignantly when they find males guffawing over, or making jokes about the subject.

Perhaps that explains why men take great delight in limericks about farting women. Note that most of these limericks are unfortunate putdowns of women.

At a flatulence contest in Butte,
One lady's exertion was cute.
It won the diploma
For fetid aroma,
And three judges were felled by the brute.

*

A certain young lady named Rowell,
Had a musical vent to her bowel.
With a good plate of beans
Tucked under her jeans,
She could play "To a Wild Rose" by MacDowell.

*

An unfortunate lass named Louise,
Unlooses huge farts with each sneeze.
She attracts quite a crowd
When they rip out so loud,
That she blushes clear down to her knees.

*

The contest for farting at Brelle,
Was won by a lady named Nell
She won the diploma
For foul aroma,
When two judges died from the smell.

*

There was a young lady from Dosset,
Who went to a pennyworth closet.*
But when she got there,
She could only puff air.
That wasn't a pennyworth, was it?

*

There was a young lady of Dorset,
Who went to an Underground closet.
She screwed up her ass
But passed only gas,
And that wasn't a tuppence-worth, was it?

*

I sat next to the Duchess at tea.
It was just as I feared it would be.
Her rumblings abdominal
Were truly phenomenal,
And everyone thought it was me!

*

The Duchess once asked with a wink,
"Pray tell me, sir, Why do farts stink?"
I quickly replied
With a smile very wide,
"For the benefit of the deaf, I think!"

*

When I thought of the duchess affair,
It suddenly struck me, "How rare
Are abnormal vitals
In ladies with titles,
So I'm glad, after all, I was there."

*

There was a young girl from La Plata,
Who was widely renowned as a farter.
Her deafening reports
At the Argentine Sports,
Makes her much in demand as a starter.

*

There was an old maid from Bruton,
Who had the bad habit of pootin'.
Her sphincter was weak,
Her wind couldn't keep,
This old spinster from Bruton was tootin'.

*

There was a young lady of France,
Supposed to play at a dance.
She ate a banana
And played the piano
And music came out of her pants.

*pennyworth closet -- a pay toilet.

◇◇◇

The macho factor...

Unlike the limericks about farting women, which largely
ridicule the female subjects, a large body of limericks about
men, some more than a century old, are testaments to
machoism. Yes, even men's farts are laced with testosterone.

I know a young fellow named Stout
Whose life is a quagmire of doubt;
He admits that he sinned
When he had to break wind
But he won't throw his windbreaker out!

*

There was a young man of Rangoon,
Who farted and filled a balloon.
The balloon went so high,
It stuck in the sky,
And stank out the Man in the Moon.
(Published 1879)

*

With his beans, Chef Richard did strive
To meet the Clean Air Standards of '95.
But his hot-start emission
Revealed a condition
Of flatulence in overdrive.

*

There once was a man from the Cape,
Whose fly was always agape.
He walked along the dunes
Singing some tunes,
Letting his flatulence escape.

*

Sir Reginald Barrington Bart,
Went to a masked ball as a fart.
He had painted his face
Like a more private place,
But his voice made the dowagers start.

*

There was a young man from Rangoon,
Whose farts could beheard to the moon.
When you'd least expect'em,
They'd boom from his rectum,
Like the roar of a double bassoon.

*

There was an old fellow named Eric,
Whose breath made those near him choleric.
He produced a hiatus,
In crowds, with his flatus.
He's a one-man disease, atmospheric.

*

An old man of Texas named Tanners,
Was notorious for his bad manners.
When he noticed the start
On an imminent fart,
He'd announce it with bullhorns and banners.

*

There was a young man from Montmartre,
Who was famed far and wide for his fart.
When they said, "What a noise!"
He replied with great poise,
When I fart, sir, I fart from the heart."

✧✧✧

The musical strains...

Given the astounding variety of sounds — from high
squealers to low oom-paas — that can emanate from the
backsides of humans, it's no wonder that dozens of limericks
of the type below have been written over the past century.

While musicians have battled for years,
Over which are the best symphoneers,
They agree from the start,
That a 'Whistling Fart'
Is great music to all of their (r)ears.

*

A German musician named Bager,
Spurred on by a very high wager,
Proceeded to fart
The complete oboe part
Of a Haydn octet in A-Major.
(Of a Mozart concerto in F-Major)

*

There once was a Royal Marine,
Who tried to fart "God save the Queen."
When he reached the soprano,
Out came the guano,
His pants were not fit to be seen.
(Published 1879)

*

A crafty old bugler of Rheims,
Would feast upon coconut creams,
And fart a toccata,
Or a Mozart sonata,
On seventeenth-century themes.

*

Don Ventouso, a stout troubadour
Wrote bad cansos; his singing was poor.
But by mastering the art
Of the audible fart,
He was able to book a long tour.

*

There once was a young man from Sparta,
A really magnificent farter.
On the strength of one bean,
He'd fart God Save The Queen,
And Beethoven's Moonlight Sonata.

*

He could vary, with proper persuasion,
His fart to suit any occasion.
He could fart like a flute,
Like a lark, like a lute,
This highly fartistic Caucasian.

81   *

This sparkling young farter from Sparta,
His fart, for no money could barter.
He could roar from his rear,
Any scene from Shakespeare,
Or Gilbert and Sullivan's Mikado.

*

His repertoire ranged from classics to jazz,
He achieved new effects using bubbles of gas.
With a good dose of salts,
He could whistle a waltz,
Or swing it in razzamatazz.

*

His basso profundo, so rare,
He rendered with power to spare.
But his great work of art,
His fortissimo fart,
He saved for the March Militaire.

*

One day he was asked to perform,
The William Tell Overture Storm.
But naught could dishearten
Our flatulent Spartan,
For his fart was in wonderful form.

*

It went off in capital style,
And he farted it through with a smile.
Then, feeling quite jolly,
He tried the finale,
Blowing double-stopped farts all the while.

✧✧✧

82

The somewhat confused...

There once was a wonderful wizard,
Who got a fierce pain in his gizzard,
So he drank wind and snow
At fifty below,
And farted a forty-day blizzard.

✧✧✧

This is not a limerick, but a song. Yes, folks, a song you can sing at your very next party. Get out the guitar and accompany yourself as you warble...

One (the Fart Song)
to the tune of "One" from "A Chorus Line"
www.netaxs.com\nukefish

One single flatulation, every bit of wind I break,
One gaseous concentration, everytime that I make,
One whiff and suddenly everyone leaves the room,
Sometimes they happen in silence or just go boom,

One single flatulation, really goes a long way,
So don't forget to cut the cheese today,
Ain't no use in tryin' to fight 'em, it's a lot of fun to light 'em,
Here comes one.

One anal exhalation, bubbles forming in the bath,
Now my diet's full of fiber, you best stay out of my path,
They are especially potent when I eat beans,
And often when I am sick they stick to my jeans,

One single flatulation, stuttering right past my cheek,
I really love to hear my rectum speak,
When I really have a zinger, I get someone to pull my finger,
Here comes one.

One single flatulation, makes the elevator reek,
They come in many flavors, every one is unique,
For sure the dog will be blamed when a girl expels,
And when ol' Grandpa explodes how the odor dwells,

One single flatulation, guaranteed to make your day,
So keep the Lysol close at hand and spray,
When I'm clever with my pushin', I sound just like a whoopee cushion,
Here comes, here comes, here comes one!

✧✧✧

PRODUCTS

(Whoopie cushions and more.)

Whoopie cushions have been with us for a long time. I suspect that back in prehistoric time, some guy named Gronk filled a mountain goat's bladder with air, constricted the opening with a twist of rawhide, hid the contraption under some bear skins at the mouth of his cave, waited for a gathering of the clan, and then tricked brother Kraak into sitting on it – much to the merriment of all the kinfolk.

You can buy a modern plastic version at most novelty stores to embarrass your own brother in front of the entire family at the very next party. But wait, there's more. Here are a few pitches from manufacturers of new novelty items.

The Original Uncle George's Fart Machine

The Ho-Ho Company makes the following claims for The original Uncle George's Fart Machine
* Hours of odorless fun
* More convincing than the real thing
* Guarantees personal space
* An ingenious amusement device affording total control
  (not a cushion)
* The perfect present

✧✧✧

Smart bomb? What about the fart bomb?

What happens when you combine a bomb bag with a stink bomb? You have an exploding bag of stuff that makes a loud noise and smells bad afterwards. This space-age foil packaging doesn't contain tang. Inside is the makings of fart bomb, just like your body reacts to pop rocks & Pepsi, this is an explosion waiting to happen.

✧✧✧

Fart Spray

Smelly stuff in a convenient, easy to use and dispense spray container. More effective than mace in avoiding people. If you want to make something smell bad just aim, shoot and spray.

✧✧✧

Fartalis

Stop fart odors with Fartalis. Fartalis stops bedroom odors before you can smell'em. A cushion-like material that you place in a pillow and then sit or lie on. Odors can't break out.

✧✧✧

Lost Recording of the First International Farting Contest

About 4o years ago some very zany radio personalities recorded the First International Crepitation (loud body function) Contest. Never released to the mass market because of its (gaseous) content, this rare recording has survived because its just too funny to "waft" away. The world championship pits champion, Lord Windesmere of Whopping Foghole, England, against the cabbage-loving challenger, Paul Boomer. Available on CD or cassette.

✧✧✧

Jurassic Farts T-shirts

This shirt is so unbelievably funny. Just looking at the squatting legs and butt on that dinosaur will crack you up.

✧✧✧

Fartology 101 T-shirts

Designed to look like a page torn out of the course catalogue or directory:

Course Number:	Fartology 101
Course Title:	Introduction to Farts
Professor:	Dr. Rex Breefs
Credits:	(3)
Description:	An overview of Flatus.
Topics include:	Intro to Farts, The Farters Diet, Fart Analysis, History of Farts and Farting, Seven Habits of Highly Flatulent People, Rectal Control, Farting Mechanics & Chemistry, The Risk of Sphincter Damage, Lighting Farts, Farts & Society, Farts in the 20th Century and Beyond
Date & Time:	Everyday after lunch
Grading:	Pass/Fail (If you don't pass gas, you fail).
Registration:	Call the fart line or register on-line

✧✧✧

American Flatulators Video

This is 55 minutes of hilarious fart-filled fun. In celebration of the popular "Gladiators" programs on television today, the parody joins Ben Dover and Big Bill Butts as they welcome the most noxious of our nation's competitors, The American Flatulators.

✧✧✧

The Fart Line Novelty Matchbooks

These real matchbooks have many fart-related uses. We can only warn you to be careful when lighting your farts. Matches may also be used to burn off the smell of other peoples farts.

✧✧✧

Fart Powder - just add water

Add this powder to your victims drink and the fireworks will begin in minutes. You can even use it on yourself. You can throw a party with all your friends and give new meaning to spiking the punch.

✧✧✧

The Fart Whistle

Use this whistle to simulate fart sounds. Effective but not as discreet.

✧✧✧

Fart Plugs

Harness the power of your farts. Use these to keep your farts bottled up until your ready to let them fly.

✧✧✧

Farting Cans

These soft plastic squeeze toys make a fart noise when you squeeze them. Hours of fun and education for your children. Teach your child the different fart nuances, including the "zipper" and the "flutter-blast." Specify whether you want the Beer can or the Bean can.

✧✧✧

The Fart Machine

A remotely controlled battery operated wonder can make anyone the butt of your evil and sick sense of humor. Attach the device to the bottom of your victims chair and you keep the remote. Whenever you hit the magic button, whammo.

✧✧✧

Le Farter

Keep this in your pocket and you can "fart" anytime. Sounds so real, people will actually think they smell something. May be used in conjunction with the Fart Spray to stimulate the "total flatulence experience."

✧✧✧

Farting Candies

Tastes like farts.

✧✧✧

Fart Sludge

Texture between "Slime" and "Silly Putty," pushing the sludge into the canister, the air inside is forced out which makes it great for fart sounds. The most real sounding farts you'll ever hear.

✧✧✧

Flatulence Detector

The detection device really works. It features a test/reset button. Fart Gas Indicator Light and a Voice Siren Alarm. Now you can be protected against miasmic and possibly dangerous human methane emanations in: elevators, public transit, restaurant, your office.

✧✧✧

The Fart Filter

The Fart Filter with activated carbon fits snugly into your underwear, discreetly blocking out the fart smells.

✧✧✧

A FINAL WORD
(Haazummmp)

In a world of information overload and rapid communications, the subject of farting is still not well understood or documented. It remains in the closet, which is where most people would like to keep it. Yet there is hope. A few brave souls have devoted time, money and imagination to publish pages on the World Wide Web devoted to the fart.

One such web site is Club Methane, which bills itself tongue-in-cheek (oops!) as The Original Support Group for the Profoundly Flatulent.

The page authors take issue with the unkind humor associated with the "profoundly flatulent."

"We've all heard unkind and insensitive comments like...Who died? ...killed the canary? ...lit the bomb? ...shot the duck? ...cut the cheese? ...you voted for who?

"For too many years we have put up with these injustices and been victimized by society," the club complains. "It's time to unite with a sense of pride in what we are...after all, what's a little gas among friends?

"It's clear, we're here, get used to it. We are mothers, fathers, sons and daughters, friends and neighbors. We are doctors, lawyers, teachers, carpenters, nurses, truck drivers and priests. We come in all shapes and sizes, all colors, all creeds and all sexual persuasions. Before you put us down, look around you. Here we are. Next to you on a bus, on an elevator, perhaps even in your own home or office..."

91

Why does a simple product of our biological function elicit both embarrassment (on the part of the perpetrator) and unkind humor (on the part of the victims). We can only conclude that the source of both is: funny noise and/or funny smell.

Club methane has its work cut out for it.

✧✧✧

GLOSSARY

The following lists were plagiarized from several sources and will help you identify various types of common, and not-so-common farts.

The anticipated fart. Sits back waiting for a time before it arrives. A person who farts at a time when he thinks no one will notice, has farted an anticipated fart.

The back seat fart. This fart occurs in automobiles, its sound concealed by traffic noise, but its odor easily distinguishable from exhaust fumes.

The barred owl fart. A familiarity with owl calls is helpful in identifying this fart. Almost any morning if you get up just before daybreak you can hear one of these birds talking to himself. It's a sort of a crazy laugh, particularly the way it ends. If you hear a fart that has about eight notes in it, ending on a couple of down notes, and it sounds maniacal, you have heard the rare barred owl fart.

The bullet fart. Its single and most pronounced characteristic is its sound. It sounds like a rifle shot. The farter can be said to have snapped it off. It can startle spectators and farter alike. Fairly common following the eating of the more common fart foods, such as beans.

The command fart. This fart differs from the anticipated fart in that it can be held for long periods of time waiting for the right moment. Unlike the anticipated fart, it is intended to be noticed.

93

The common fart. This fart needs little description. It is to the world of farts what the house sparrow is to the world of birds. There is no point in describing this far any further.

The cushioned fart. A concealed fart, sometimes successful. The farter is usually on the large side, sometimes a woman. They will squirm and push their butt way down into the cushions of a sofa or over-stuffed chair and ease-out a fart very carefully without moving then or for some time after. Some odor may escape, but usually not much. Common with some people.

The dud fart. The dud fart is not really a fart at all. It's a fart that fails. For this reason it is strictly a group one identification fart, because there is no real way you can identify a fart that somebody else expected to fart but didn't. It is the most private of all farts. In most cases the farter usually feels a little disappointed.

The echo fart. This is a fart that can be wrongly identified. It is not some great loud fart in an empty gym or on the rim of the Grand Canyon. The true echo fart is a fart that makes its own echo. It is a two-toned fart, the first tone loud, then a pause, and then the second tone. Like an echo.

The G and L fart. This is one of the most ordinary and pedestrian of farts, known to everyone. Certainly it is the least gross. If you have not already guessed, G and L stands for Gambled and Lost. One of the most embarrassing of all farts, even when you are alone.

The ghost fart. A doubtful fart in most cases, as it is supposed to be identified by odor alone and to occur, for instance, in an empty house. You enter and smell a fart, yet no one is there. People will insist that only a fart could have that odor, but some believe it is just something that happens to smell like a fart.

The hic-hachoo-fart fart. This is strictly an old lady's fart. What happens is that the person manages to hiccough, sneeze, and fart all at the same time. After an elderly lady farts a hic-hachoo-fart fart she will usually pat her chest and say, "My, my", or "Well, well". There is no reason she should not be proud, as this is probably as neat an old person's fart as there is.

The jerk fart. The jerk fart is a fart by a jerk who smirks, smiles, grins, and points to himself in case you missed it. It is usually a single-noted, off-key, fading away, sort of whistle fart, altogether pitiful, but the jerk will act as if he has just farted the biggest-fart-in-the-world fart.

The john fart. The John Fart is simply any ordinary fart farted on the john. It is naturally a group one identification, with the sound, whatever it was, somewhat muffled. If it is all the person's trip to the john amounted to he will be disappointed for sure. Common as pigeons.

The lead fart. The heaviest of all farts. It sounds like a dropped ripe watermelon. Or a falling body in some cases. It is the only fart that goes thud. Except for the odor, which is also very heavy, it could be missed altogether as a fart. What was that, you might think? And never guess.

The malted milk ball fart. Odor alone is diagnostic and positively identifies this fart. It smells exactly like malted milk balls. No other food works this way. It is rare.

The oh-my-God fart. This is the most awful and dreadful stinking of all farts - a fart that smells like a month-old rotten egg - as the Oh My God Fart. If you should ever encounter it, however, you may first want to say, oh shit, which would be understandable.

95

The omen fart. This is the adult version of the poo-poo fart. About the only difference is that the farter will not say anything. He will just look kind of funny and head for the john. This one is easy to spot if you pay attention.

The organic fart. Sometimes called the health food nut fart. The person who farts an organic fart may be talking about the healthy food he eats even when he farts. If he is heavily into health foods he may even ask if you noticed how good and pure and healthy his fart smells. It may smell to you like any other fart, but there is no harm in agreeing with him. He is doing what he thinks is best.

The quiver fart. A group one identification fart only. When you fart, it quivers. If it tickles, then it is the tickle fart. If you have to scratch it, then it is the scratchass fart.

The rambling phaduka fart. You must not be fooled by its pretty-sounding name, as this is one of the most frightening of all farts. It is frightening to farter and spectator alike. It has a sound of pain to it. What is most diagnostic about it, however, is its length. It is the longest-lasting fart there is. It will sometimes leave the farter unable to speak. As though he has had the wind knocked out of him. A strong, loud, wavering fart, it goes on for at least fifteen seconds.

The relief fart. Sound or odor don't matter on this one. What matters is the tremendous sense of relief that you have finally farted. Some people will even say, "Wow, what a relief". Very common.

The reluctant fart. This is probably one of the oldest farts known to man. The reluctant fart is a fart that seems to have a mind of its own. It gives the impression that it likes staying where it is. It will come when it is ready, not before. This can take half-a-day in some instances.

The rusty gate fart. The sound of this fart seems almost impossible for a fart. It's the most dry and squeaky sound a fart can make. The rusty gate fart sounds as if it would have worked a lot easier if it had been oiled. It sounds like a fart that hurts.

The S.B.D. fart. S.B.D. stands for silent but deadly. This is no doubt one of the most common farts that exists. No problem of identification with this one.

The sandpaper fart. This one scratches. Otherwise it may not amount to much. You should remember that if you reach back and scratch, it automatically becomes a scratchass fart.

The skillsaw fart. A truly awesome fart. It vibrates the farter. Really shakes him up. People back away. It sounds like an electric skillsaw ripping through a piece of half-inch plywood. Very impressive. Not too common.

The sonic boom fart. The people who believe in this fart claim it is even bigger than the biggest-fart-in-the-world fart. The sonic boom fart is supposed to shake the house and rattle the windows. This is ridiculous. No fart in the world shakes houses and rattles windows. A fart that could do that would put the farter into orbit or blow his crazy head off.

The splatter fart. Unfortunately the splatter fart exists. It is the wettest of all farts. It probably should not be called a fart at all.

The stutter fart. If you think stuttering is funny, this is a very funny fart. It is a fart that can't seem to get going. The sound is best described as pt,pt,pt-pt,pt-pt-pt,pop,pop-pop-pop-POW! It is usually a forced-out fart that gets caught crossways, as they say, and only gets farted after considerable effort.

The Taco Bell fart. The Taco Bell fart is far richer and full-bodied than your ordinary fart and takes longer to build up. Sometimes hours or even a day. But it will get there. And it will hang around after, too, even on a windy day.

The Teflon fart. Slips out without a sound and no strain at all. A very good fart in situations where you would rather not fart at all. You can be talking to someone and not miss saying a word. If the wind is right he will never know.

The thank God I'm alone fart. Everyone knows this rotten fart. You look around after you have farted and say thank God I'm alone. Then you get out of there.

97

THE FART CHART

Ambitious	Always ready for a fart
Amiable	Likes to smell others' farts
Anti-Social	Excuses himself and farts in private
Aquatic	Farts in the bathtub then breaks the -bubbles with his toes
Athletic	Jumps in the air, farts 3 times, and kicks his heels 3 times
Bewildered	Can't tell his own farts from others
Big Bully	Farts louder than others
Careless	Farts in church
Childish	Farts then giggles
Clever	Farts and coughs at the same time
Conceited	Thinks he can fart the loudest
Confused	Face is so much like the butt, fart can't tell which way to go
Cute	Smells your farts and then tells you what you were eating
Damned Mean	Farts then pulls the covers over his wife's head
Dishonest	Farts then blames the dog
Disappointed	Fart doesn't smell
Dumb	Enjoys others farts, thinks they are his own
Environmentalist	Farts regularly but is concerned about the pollution
Foolish	Suppresses a fart for hours
Fresh Guy	Jumps in front of you then farts
Grouch	Grumbles when ladies fart

Honest	Admits he farted but offered a good medical reason
Impudent	Farts out loud then laughs
Lazy	Just fizzles
Masochist	Farts in the bathtub and tries to bite the bubbles
Miserable	Can't fart at all
Musical	Tenor or Bass, Clear as a bell
Nervous	Stops in the middle of a fart
Proud	Thinks his farts are exceptionally pleasant
Sadist	Farts in bed then fluffs the covers
Scientific	Bottles his farts
Sensitive	Farts then starts crying
Shy	Blushes when he farts silently
Slob	Farts and stains his underwear
Smart Alec	Farts when ladies are present
Sneaky	Farts and blames it on the dog
Stingy	Belches to save his other orifice
Strategic	Conceals his fart by loud laughter
Thrifty	One who always has farts in reserve
Timid	Jumps when he farts
Unfortunate	Tries to fart but shits himself
Vain Person	One who loves the smell of his own fart
Wimpy	Farts at the slightest exertion

ANOTHER LIST

Amiable person   One who loves the smell of other people's farts.

Anti-social person   One who excuses himself and farts in complete privacy.

Aquatic person   One who farts in the bath then bursts the bubbles with his toes.

Athletic person   One who farts at the slightest exertion.

Dishonest person   One who farts and blames the dog.

Foolish person   One who suppresses a fart for hours.

Honest person   One who admits he has farted but offers a good medical reason.

Impudent person   One who farts out loud then laughs.

Intellectual person One who can determine the smell of his neighbour's farts.

Miserable person   One who truly enjoys a fart but cannot.

Nervous person   One who stops in the middle of a fart.

Proud person   One who thinks his farts are exceptionally good.

Sadistic person	One who farts in bed and fluffs the covers over his bed mate.
Scientific person	One who farts regularly but is concerned about pollution.
Sensitive person	One who farts then starts crying.
Shy person	One who releases a fart then blushes.
Strategic person	One who conceals a fart by loud laughter.
Thrifty person	One who always has farts in reserve.
Unfortunate person	One who tries to fart but shits instead.
Vain person	One who loves the smell of his own fart.